How to Pass the Garda Recruitment Process

Expert Advice from Former Garda Superintendent Noel McLoughlin

MASTER EACH STAGE OF THE RECRUITMENT PROCESS AND LAND YOUR DREAM JOB IN AN GARDA SÍOCHÁNA

ORLA KELLY PUBLISHING

Noel McLoughlin

Noel-John McLoughlin

Orla Kelly Publishing
27 Kilbrody,
Mount Oval,
Rochestown,
Cork

Disclaimer

The content of this book is for general information purposes only. While every effort has been made to ensure the accuracy of this information, readers should consult with the Public Appointments Service or An Garda Síochána before acting on any such information.

No liability is assumed by the authors for any losses suffered directly or indirectly by any person relying on the information contained in this book.

Changes, corrections, and improvements will be incorporated in new versions, at any time without notice.

About the Authors

Former Garda Superintendent **Noel McLoughlin** established GardaIP in 2006. Since then, GardaIP has grown to become the premier and most trusted source for Garda Entry Preparation coaching and tuition.

A native of Westport County Mayo, Noel retired from An Garda Síochána after a distinguished career. He served at various ranks in the Dublin Metropolitan Area, and in Divisions of Cavan/Monaghan, Cork, Westmeath, Garda HQ, and Community Relations.

He was a member of the Garda Interview Panel at the Public Appointments Service (PAS) since its inception in 1996.

Noel also served on numerous interview boards for internal appointments within the organisation. He is a past President of the Association of Garda Superintendents and has had extensive media exposure throughout his career. He is a regular contributor to national media discussions on the Garda Recruitment process and has featured on RTE TV and RTE Radio, TV3, Today FM, and Newstalk.

Noel is passionate about helping his clients achieve their dream of becoming members of An Garda Síochána. Anybody that he has tutored or prepared will attest to how much additional guidance, advice and support he provides to applicants.

Noel-John McLoughlin established Garda Interview Preparation www.gardaip.com in 2006. Holding an EMCC accredited Advanced

Diploma in Executive Coaching, McLoughlin has mentored and prepared a significant number of candidates for both public and private sector appointments specialising in matching competencies against individual skill sets and personal achievements.

Noel-John McLoughlin is qualified to British Psychological Society standards in Psychometric Testing. He has tutored candidates for Aptitude Tests and Competency Interviews from recruitment level to senior management positions in large public and private sector organisations.

Noel-John has held senior marketing and commercial positions with L'Oréal, Britvic, and Fáilte Ireland.

He holds a Bachelor of Business and Law from UCD, a Masters in Marketing from the Michael Smurfit School of Business, and a Diploma in Digital Marketing from the Marketing Institute of Ireland. Noel-John was also nominated by Business and Finance magazine as one of the top 100 Marketers in Ireland.

About GardaIP

To find out more about the courses we offer in Garda Trainee preparation, please go to GardaIP.com. While there, feel free to download our complimentary guide for trainees and sign up for expert videos delivered to your email inbox. They cover a diverse range of topics you will not want to miss if you are serious about becoming a Garda.

Dedication

We dedicate this book to all those who have worked, are currently working, or hope to work in An Garda Síochána.

Contents

Introduction

So, you want to join An Garda Síochána? You have been thinking about it for a long time and decided that now is the time is right to go for it. Excellent!

When you reach that point, it can be an exciting time and you probably want to get started sooner rather than later, because the faster you get the ball rolling the quicker you'll be accepted.

Applying to join An Garda Síochána is what I call a middle-distance race rather than a 100m sprint.

It is, in fact, a very competitive process where only a small fraction of applicants end up being successful.

So, what is the secret to success? One word: **Preparation**.

Well good news, you are now holding the right book in your hand. This book is born out of the scar tissue of the thousands of individuals that I have coached and prepared through the Garda Recruitment Process over the years.

I am committed to helping you achieve your dream career in An Garda Síochána.

Let me introduce myself:

My name is Noel McLoughlin and I spent 40 years as a member of An Garda Síochána. I served at various ranks to the rank of Superintendent in the Dublin Metropolitan Area, and in Divisions of Cavan/Monaghan, Cork, Westmeath, Garda Headquarters, and Community Relations.

I was a member of the Garda Interview Panel at the Public Appointments Service (PAS) since its inception in 1996. I also served on numerous interview boards for internal appointments in the organisation.

I am a past President of the Association of Garda Superintendents, and am a regular contributor to national media discussions on the Garda Recruitment process and have featured on RTE Television and RTE Radio, TV3, Today FM, and Newstalk.

Let me take you back a few years when I was sitting on the Garda Interview Panel at the Public Appointments Service.

I absolutely loved my work on the panel. I got to meet and interview candidates from diverse backgrounds, unique experiences, and from towns and villages all over Ireland. As rewarding as this role was, I often felt frustrated.

I was frustrated because I interviewed some outstanding candidates, who would have made fine Gardai, but were unfortunately unsuccessful with their Garda application.

To put in simply, they were underprepared. In a highly competitive entry process, they left their performance on the day to chance. My frustration was born out of the fact that the unsuccessful candidate did not have access to a specialist resource to optimise their performance at each stage of the recruitment process. By 'specialist resource' I mean somebody that has not only worn the Garda uniform, but also served on boards and sat on interview panels at the Public Appointments Service.

As far as An Garda Síochána are concerned, they would much prefer that candidates approach each stage of the recruitment process with the same level of prior knowledge. Their argument is that each candidate is starting on an equal footing.

No apologies. This thinking really goes against one of my core values – the value of preparation. I was raised by my parents on this value, I passed it on to my children, my teammates when I was playing sport, and of course my staff and colleagues when I was a serving member of An Garda Síochána. No half measures. Always put your full self into all your endeavours. You can have no regrets if you put the hard graft in.

This core value is what led my son, Noel-John, and I to create GardaIP, when I retired from An Garda Síochána. We wanted to provide specialist and expert guidance and coaching to candidates applying for a career in An Garda Síochána. So, in 2007 GardaIP was born. Since then, we have successfully prepared thousands of candidates at entry level, internal promotion at all ranks, and for specialist positions in An Garda Síochána.

How can this book help you?

The purpose of this book is to get you 'Competition Fit' for the Garda Recruitment process. Written from an insider perspective, this book takes you through all the requirements you need to pass recruitment from the application to the competency-based interview.

It is written in a very easy-to-read style and follows the sequence and format of the Garda Recruitment process as it exists today.

In this book I will share our expertise to help you better navigate the Garda application process, help you maximise your applicant score at Stages 1, 2, and 3 and improve your chances of achieving your dream of joining An Garda Síochána.

You will find explanations of the thinking behind each stage of the recruitment process. We will help you understand the background to each stage, gain an insight into what the assessors are looking for and why, drill down into the mechanics of each exercise, set out some practice tests for you, and give you our insights and expert tips throughout each chapter.

Our Promise to You

The purpose of this book is to help you become the best you can be in what is always a competitive field. If you understand the process and what they are looking for - you are halfway to achieving the score required to pass each stage of the process. With proper preparation, you will achieve a score much higher than required, placing you higher than your peers in the Order of Merit.

If I could guarantee that you will be accepted into the Garda Training

College at Templemore if you followed everything suggested in the following pages, then the price of this book would be a lot higher! However, the assurance that I can give you is that if you use the advice and suggestions given here you will significantly boost your chances of success.

When you follow the advice, ideas, concepts, and expertise in this book you will be in control of how you approach the completion of the Application Form, the Stage 1 Online Assessment, the Stage 2 Supervised Assessment, and the Stage 3 Competency Interview.

My advice is to follow this maxim:

'If it is going to be, it is down to me.'

You are in the driving seat. We are simply providing you with directions and guidance. We can promise you that if you work hard at your preparation, it will increase your confidence levels, and will naturally boost your chances of achieving your dream career.

Let us get started…

Chapter 1

An Overview of the Garda Recruitment Process

How do I join An Garda Síochána?

This is the most common question we are asked at GardaIP, hands down. The truth is that the initial stages can be overwhelming and you may be concerned about missing out on some of the finer detail.

Let us address this now.

The competition for the selection of Garda Trainees attracts an extremely high number of applicants – each campaign typically attracts more than 7,000 applications. Naturally, these numbers increase in the years where there is no recruitment campaigns. For example, in 2014, more than 20,000 candidates applied for 300 positions – these were exceptional circumstances as there was a recruitment freeze for the previous four years.

Unsurprisingly, the selection process to become a Garda Trainee is comprehensive, with candidates required to undertake a range of relevant assessment tests and exercises over several selection stages. The tests and exercises are designed to identify candidates suitable to be a Garda Trainee, with potential to become an attested member – this means a Garda regardless of rank who has completed the training, taken the requisite oath, and has been listed in the force as a member.

Therefore, only the highest performing candidates at each stage will progress to the next stage. The numbers called forward to each stage of selection will be determined from time to time having regard to the number of places to be filled in the Garda College. The typical intake each year ranges from 500 to 800 Trainees.

The Public Appointments Service conduct the initial selection stages on behalf of the Garda Commissioner. There are three stages to this process.

What are the Eligibility Criteria for entry to An Garda Síochána*

*(note: these are the most recent eligibility criteria from The Public Appointments Service (PAS) and may be subject to change).Reference edited version of *Competition for Selection of Garda Trainees 2019, Notes for Applicants and Conditions of Service.*

To be eligible for selection as a Trainee, an applicant must:

General:

(i) Be of good character.

(ii) Be certified by a Registered Medical Practitioner to be in good health, of sound constitution and suited physically and mentally to performing the duties of a member of the Service.

(iii) Have passed a physical competence test.

Age:

(iv) Be 18 years of age but not yet 35 years of age on midnight of (*TBC – the dates depend on the closing date for applications when the campaign is announced).*

Nationality:

(v) (a) Be a national of a European Union Member State, or

(b) Be a national of a European Economic Area State or the Swiss Confederation; or

(c) Be a Refugee under the Refugee Act, 1996; or

(d) Have had a period of one year's continuous residence in the State on the closing date of the advertisement for the competition for the vacancy to which the admission relates, and during the eight years immediately preceding that period, has had a total residence in the State amounting to four years; or

(e)Has been granted subsidiary protection, or is a family member of such a person, in compliance with the Admissions and Appointments Regulations 2013.

Education:

(vi) Have by the closing date:

(a) Obtained an Irish Leaving Certificate with a grade D3 minimum in five subjects at Ordinary Level*, or

(b) hold a Level 5 Certificate (Major award) on the National Framework of Qualifications (NFQ), or

(c) hold a recognised qualification (at Level 5 or greater), deemed comparable to the above in terms of both level and volume of learning as determined by Quality and Qualifications Ireland (QQI)

Application Streams

For every recruitment campaign, there are typically three application streams. These are:

1. General
2. Fluency in the Irish Language
3. Eligible Serving Garda Reserve Members

Fluent Irish Speakers Stream

For fluent Irish speakers invited through to the final stages of the selection process you will be required to undergo certain selection elements through Irish (e.g., competency-based interview and written Irish test). You must achieve the required level (i.e., demonstrate a minimum Level B2 on the Europass self-assessment framework).

Candidates appointed from this stream must be able to provide a full range of services in Irish. If successful, candidates will be allocated to Gaeltacht areas for a period of time as determined by the Garda Commissioner.

Serving Garda Reserve Members Stream

Members of the Garda Reserve give their time on a voluntary basis to support the work of An Garda Síochána within the community. They have undergone training in many of the skills required to be an effective full-time member of An Garda Síochána and have gained experience in operational policing.

In recognition of this, a separate stream is typically held for serving Garda Reserve members who, by the closing date have:

1. Completed their probationary period

2. Performed their role to a satisfactory standard

3. Served a minimum of 120 hours per year for two of the last four claim years

4. Fulfil the Conditions for Entry

Eligible applicants should apply in the usual way and indicate on the Application Form that they wish to apply for the *Serving Garda Reserve Stream*.

In order to be considered for this stream, when completing your Application Form, you must include:

1. Garda Reserve Registration Number

2. Division in which you are currently serving

Applicants must be a member of the Garda Reserve at the time of appointment as a Garda Trainee to continue to be eligible under the Garda Reserve Stream. Applicants that are no longer a member of the Garda Reserve will not be offered an appointment from this Stream.

You should be aware that, at the time of the publication of this book, recruitment of Garda Reserves is presently on hold. pending the outcome of a comprehensive strategic review.

How long does the Recruitment Process take?

It can typically take between 12-18 months from initial application to being called for training at the Garda College, Templemore. Completing the application process does not guarantee you a place at the Garda College. All it does is get you onto a waiting list to be called onto the next Trainee Intake at Templemore.

It is important to be patient and use the time in between each process to study and prepare or the next stage. This also includes fitness training, in preparation for the fitness test which is usually undertaken towards the end of the process.

The Application process consists of five stages. Of those that apply, typically only between 5-10% of applicants are successful at becoming a Garda and many have had to apply several times before being successful.

If you do not succeed on your first attempt, ensure you get feedback on your scores from the PAS and then re-apply when the next campaign is announced. Do not get disheartened – use your learnings from your previous experience.

Reading this book alone will ensure you are better prepared than most of those that apply.

Register with Public Jobs

The very first step to applying to An Garda Síochána is to register your interest through the Public Appointments Service on www. publicjobs.ie.

Candidates should not confuse registering (i.e., creating a profile on publicjobs.ie) with submitting an application. Once you have created a profile you must then access the application form, complete, and submit it. The Public Appointments Service is the centralised recruiter for An Garda Síochána and they will process the candidates on their behalf.

When the campaign is announced you will receive a comprehensive document called Notes for Candidates and Conditions of Service. In short, this document covers all the essential detail you need to navigate the recruitment process.

Let us cover the most relevant detail now. I have summarised it as follows:

How to Register with Public Jobs for An Garda Síochána:

Now, let us talk about the admin. This is hugely important – if you miss the announcement of the campaign you will have to wait until the following year. If you submit incomplete detail, it may delay your application or even disqualify you! This detail is always set out in the Garda Trainee Notes for Applicants. As mentioned earlier, the Public Appointments Service (PAS) publish this document in advance of every Garda recruitment campaign.

This is what you need to know:

Applications should be made online to the Public Appointments Service through its website www.publicjobs.ie. It is recommended that applicants do not use a tablet (iPad) or mobile device to apply. Therefore, it is advisable for you to complete this detail on a laptop.

To apply, candidates must have a 'User Account' on www.publicjobs. ie. If you have not already done so, you must register as a 'New User' to create your profile (register a new account). If you cannot remember your profile details from before, please do not create a second profile as this could nullify your application.

Candidates should not confuse registering (creating a profile) with applying. Once you have created a profile you must then access the Application Form, complete and submit it.

Candidates must use their own valid email address. Email addresses from third parties will not be accepted and may invalidate your application.

The Public Appointments Service will send most communication through your public jobs message board. You are advised to check your Messageboard on a regular basis as email notifications of updates/tests issued to your Messageboard can sometimes be filtered into your Junk/Spam email folders. This is extremely important – we have had candidates contact us to say that they missed key dates for Stage 2 and even the Stage 3 Interview – they were subsequently disqualified from that year's competition!

How to Apply to An Garda Síochána:

When the Minister for Justice announces a Garda Recruitment campaign, here are the steps you need to take:

1. Access the job posting by clicking on the 'Garda Trainee' link (when its live) on the home page of www.publicjobs.ie.

2. Click on the button 'Apply Now' to access the Application Form. This button is located at the end of the job posting page. You must complete the Application Form in full and click the submit button. We will cover the Application Form in more detail in the next chapter.

3. Once you have submitted your Application Form you should return to your publicjobs account and confirm that it has been successfully submitted via 'My Applications'.

4. At this point, you should consider adding www.publicjobs. ie to your safe senders or contact list within your email account to avoid not receiving emails because a publicjobs email has been blocked.

5. Remember to always include your PPS number when applying.

STEPS IN THE APPLICATION PROCESS

APPLICATION FORM

STAGE 1 UNSUPERVISED ONLINE ASSESSMENTS

STAGE 2 SUPERVISED ONLINE ASSESSMENTS

STAGE 3 COMPETENCY BASED INTERVIEW

MEDICAL ASSESSMENT

FITNESS TEST

VETTING / BACKGROUND CHECK

The Steps in the Recruitment Process

The Application Form

Writing your Application is the first step of a long process when applying to join An Garda Síochana, and it is where many people unwittingly let themselves down!

I cannot emphasize enough the importance of preparing a well-constructed and professional Garda Trainee Application Form. The form provides you with a gilt-edged opportunity to present your personal achievements to date that demonstrates the competencies and necessary skills and qualities required for a career in An Garda Síochána.

In the Application Form you must provide details on:

- Academic, professional, or technical qualifications: second level / third level / professional / qualifications plus results attained.

- Employment history: Starting with your present or most recent employment you must briefly describe your role and responsibilities.

- Voluntary or community work: You must provide detail of any voluntary or community work you have done which relates to the role of Garda Trainee.

- Hobbies and interests: You must list any hobbies or interests which may be relevant to the role of Garda Trainee.

- Supplementary information: This section provides an opportunity to detail any other relevant information in support of your application.

I will cover the Application Form in much greater detail in Chapter 2.

Stage 1 Online Assessment

The Stage 1 Online Assessment of the competition is an unsupervised assessment which you will take at home.

This assessment includes:

- Assessment Questionnaire
- Logical Reasoning Test
- Verbal Reasoning Test

Your result in these tests decides your placing (referred to as the Order of Merit i.e., OOM) on the list of candidates.

If you are thinking about taking this assessment without preparing properly to see how you go, you have missed the point about the importance of getting your best score and boosting your position on the Order of Merit.

I will cover the Stage 1 Online Assessment in much greater detail in Chapter 3.

Stage 2 Assessment

The Stage 2 Assessment is a repeat of Stage 1 in a supervised environment along with two additional Tests. The assessment typically takes place at the PAS Head Office in Dublin.

Stage 2 is made up of the following assessments:

- Re-test of the two Aptitude Tests undertaken in the first stage (i.e., Verbal Reasoning and Logical Reasoning)
- Job Simulation Exercises
- Report Writing Exercise

The test is conducted in supervised conditions to ensure that candidates did not cheat when attempting the Stage1 online assessments without supervision!

The failure rate in these tests is high. Your result in these tests decides your placing on the list of candidates and dictates where you are placed in the Order of Merit. The higher you score, the faster the turnaround in time to your Stage 3 Competency Interview.

I will cover the Stage 2 supervised assessment in much greater detail in Chapter 4.

Stage 3 Competency Based Interview

Stage 3 is a formal Competency Based Interview. The competencies, which are predefined by the three person interview board, are key skills deemed necessary to serve effectively as a member of An Garda Síochána.

The Interview typically lasts 45 minutes and typically takes place at the PAS Head Office in Dublin. Going forward it may be conducted online.

It is an examination of five competencies. Be aware that your interview will also focus on the content in your Application Form to examine these competencies.

The five competencies are:

1. Exercising Authority

2. Resilience

3. Conscientiousness

4. Interpersonal Skills and Service Ethos

5. Using Information and Problem Solving

Note: These are the most recent competencies based on Garda Trainee Competition 2019 and may be subject to change by the PAS.

During the interview candidates are asked to give examples of instances when they displayed each of the competencies effectively. Most people choose examples from their previous work experience, voluntary experience, educational experience, or a hobby that they enjoy.

I will cover the Stage 3 Competency Interview in much greater detail in Chapter 5.

Stage 4 Medical Examination

Stage 4 is the Garda Medical examination. Successful applicants from Stage 3 will also be required to undergo a comprehensive medical examination by a Registered Medical Practitioner nominated by the Commissioner of An Garda Síochána. Applicants must be of good mental and bodily health and free from any defect or abnormality likely to interfere with the efficient performance of their duties.

If you are successful at the Competency Interview and pass your Medical Assessment you will called forward to complete the Fitness Test.

Stage 5 Fitness Test

The Fitness Test is comprised of two separate stages. The idea of the test is to test your endurance and dynamic strength.

The tests are all tailored and evaluated against your age category and gender. The two stages are:

Fitness Test – three components:

Progressive shuttle run

Sit-up test (one minute time limit)

Press-up test (no time limit)

Physical Competence Test – two components:

Competency-based timed circuit (three sets / laps)

Push/Pull machine assessment

If you do not pass on the first attempt, talk to the fitness instructor for a training plan to get you up to speed. **You can retake your fitness test** – better to start getting your fitness built up now!

The Background Check

Naturally, An Garda Síochána are looking for applicants who are of good character and reputation.

Once you have passed the Competency Based Interview you will asked to complete and submit Form B – this is the form that forms the basis of your background check.

This includes all places that you resided, names and addresses of all your blood relations up to your grandparents, and details of any dealings you may have had with An Garda Síochána including any previous offences.

In terms of background checks, if you have lived overseas, those background checks will take longer than they might for an applicant who's lived only in Ireland, has less offences, less criminal convictions, and so on.

Part of checking into your background will include checks around your social media activity. You have got to be very careful about how you use social media. This avenue gives a real insight as to what you are really like, rather than what you present yourself to be in your application.

The background check is often the slowest part of the entire application process. You will need to be patient, but most of all honest.

My advice is that you can help speed things up by getting information ready in advance. Again, family names and addresses, references, any prior offences, associations with people 'of concern'. Get all this information ready to go.

Do you still want to join An Garda Síochána? Of course, you do! Now let us delve into the Application Form in greater detail.

Chapter 2

The Application Form

Why is the Application Form so important?

I cannot emphasise enough the importance of preparing a well-constructed and professional Garda Trainee Application Form. So many times, candidates have contacted me after they have submitting their form wishing they had invested more time in its preparation.

The form provides you with a gilt-edged opportunity to present your personal achievements to date that demonstrates the skills and qualities required for a career in An Garda Síochána.

The Application Form is the first chance An Garda Síochána has at seeing what you are all about. There are no rules around how much information you include on the form. My advice is to include as much detail as possible – why sell yourself short?

Did you know that at the Stage 3 Competency Interview, the Board will have a copy of your Application Form and may refer to it during your interview? The interview board has no prior knowledge of your career or academic history, therefore, the onus is on you to include all relevant information. Any information you include is often discussed in more depth at the interview.

So many candidates leave the completion of the Application Form to the night before the submission deadline, rush the detail, leave out critical information, and make spelling mistakes. They quickly forget about the Application Form and move onto Stage 1 and Stage 2.

If successful at Stage 2 you are called forward to the Stage 3 Competency Interview and, as mentioned, are notified that the interview panel will refer to your application during the Interview. Panic sets in. Where is my Application Form? What detail did I provide? Why did I leave out that work experience? Why did I not provide addition information in Section C?

Attention to Detail

My advice is always the same – you should complete the Application Form with great care and attention to detail.

Remember, I sat on the interview panel at the Public Appointments Service. My view was simple. If you complete the form incorrectly, (i.e., by missing critical detail, or making spelling mistakes, or not completing the detail in the correct sequence) you are demonstrating your inability to understand basic instructions. As a Garda Trainee you will be expected to follow basic instructions – completing a form should be a hygiene factor.

Some Basic Admin Advice First

- Include your Candidate ID on the Form – applicants often forget to include it!

- All questions on the Application Form must be completed.

- If you do not complete all questions, you will **not** have the opportunity to add additional information later in the recruitment competition.

- The Application Form is a dynamic PDF e-Form which requires the free Adobe Reader to function correctly. This is important – make sure you download the latest version of Adobe Reader!

- The Application Form allows you to add sections to accommodate extra entries. You may need to do this for your employment history.

- You can copy and paste text from any other document type into the fields on the form. This is a handy function – you can copy and paste from Word docs e.g., your CV.

- The PAS recommend that you keep a copy of the Application Form for your own records. As emphasised earlier, you will need a copy of the Form if called for the Stage 3 Competency Interview.

- Before you return the form to the Public Appointments Service you must ensure that you have signed the declaration at the end of the form. This confirms that the information given in the form is correct and gives your permission for enquiries to be made to establish facts such as age, qualifications, experience, and character.

What detail is required on the Application Form?

The Application Form has followed the same format for the past number of years. Of course, it is subject to change, however it always seeks out information against each of these headings. You must provide details on the following:

Section A:

- ACADEMIC, PROFESSIONAL OR TECHNICAL QUALIFICATIONS: Second level / Third level / Professional / Qualifications plus results attained.

- EMPLOYMENT HISTORY: Starting with your present or most recent employment you must briefly describe your role and responsibilities.

Section B:

- VOLUNTARY / COMMUNITY WORK: You must provide detail of any voluntary or community work you have done which relates to the role of Garda Trainee.

- HOBBIES and INTERESTS: You must list any hobbies or interests which may be relevant to the role of Garda Trainee.

Section C:

- SUPPLEMENTARY INFORMATION: This section provides an opportunity to detail any other relevant information in support of your application.

Ok let us get into the detail behind each section.

The Interview will always be seeking to align your work experience with the role of a Garda Trainee!

Section A – Academic, Professional and Technical Qualifications:

In this section you must **start with your most recent qualification** then move down through the form to add more qualification records, as necessary.

You are requested to **include second-level and third level education and any other training/courses, <u>whether completed or not</u>.** This is especially important. If you have not completed your studies at college, which is common amongst applicants, you should still include details of the college, course, subjects taken, and years of study.

You must include your Leaving Certificate grades – if you do not have a record of your grades to hand then contact the Department of Education to request a copy. Do this now so you are not panicking when completing the Form!

Section A – Employment History:

In this section you must start with details of your current employment. Then, work in sequence providing **full particulars of all employment (including any periods of unemployment)**

between the date of leaving school or college and the present date.
You should always include any jobs held if you travelled abroad or
spend summers abroad on a working visa.

You must **mark if the employment is/was permanent, temporary,
or acting.**

I have spoken to numerous applicants that were uncomfortable
including periods of unemployment. My advice is not to lie or falsify
the form – the background check always reveals the truth, so be
honest.

A period of unemployment is nothing to be ashamed of and is very
common. Be prepared to talk about it in positive terms if it is raised
by the Panel at the Stage 3 Interview. You can talk about how you
worked in a voluntary capacity over this period or how you used the
time to upskill by enrolling in a course.

You will be prompted to include details of your main duties and
responsibilities. Do not gloss over this detail. Why not source your
original job description to ensure you have captured the exact detail
of your role? Do not sell yourself short here – the Interview will
always be seeking to align your work experience with the role of a
Garda Trainee!

Lastly, you will be asked you give the reason for leaving this
employment. Keep it positive. I have seen Forms where the applicants
wrote 'I did not get on with my boss' or 'the job was boring, there
was no challenge in the job for me'. Both are red flags to the Garda
Síochána, and reflect very poorly on the applicant! Keep it positive
such as 'the new opportunity offered me a greater challenge and
greater opportunity to use my customer service skills'

Section B – Voluntary / Community Work:

This is a question that you must be prepared to answer in your Application Form. It is a question that every applicant is likely to get at the Stage 3 Competency Interview, later in the selection process. In short, it is important and the interview panel attach weight to what you have written on the Form.

That question is *"Please outline details of any voluntary or community work you have done which relates to the role of Garda Trainee".*

A Garda must have a strong commitment to good public service. This is imperative because the central aim of An Garda Síochána is to work in the interests of public safety and welfare. Good public service means that you are responsible, polite, and considerate at all times. By utilising these traits, a Garda can earn the trust of the public, and enhance the reputation of An Garda Síochána as a whole.

Can you provide examples of when you helped your community or provided excellent service to an individual or group?

Volunteering, or giving up your time for the benefit of someone else is a good indicator of the type of person that you are, more so than just the Garda applicant that you are. It shows the person beneath the applicant.

So, if you are volunteering in your community, whether it is something like coaching a GAA team, fundraising for a charity, volunteering for a college event, or maybe you are involved in your Residents Committee – well that is excellent! If you are, then you'll have plenty of experiences that you can draw on to give as an example of how you like to help people and how you are community minded.

So, if you have not already started volunteering, this is something you should seriously consider because An Garda Síochána are looking for people who like helping people, who are community-minded, who like giving back.

Section B – Hobbies and Interests:

Specifically, you are asked to *"List any hobbies or interests which may be relevant to the role of Garda Trainee"*.

Again, many candidates gloss over this detail or worse, leave it blank. This section provides you with an opportunity to set yourself apart from other applicants.

My advice is to include detail of all memberships of sports and social clubs. Include your achievements with these clubs. Include your interests such as travelling, reading, etc., but expand on them. Give the detail behind the destinations you visited, the books you enjoy reading. Why? All of these are conversation starters and may pique interest in the Interview Panel.

Section C – Supplementary Information:

Specifically, the question in this section is *"Please give below any other relevant information in support of your application".*

So, you are now nearly at the end of the form – you have emptied the tank – you have given every ounce of detail on your academic history, work history, voluntary work, hobbies and interests. What could you possibly include in Section C?

Here are some considerations for you:

- Were you or are you a member of the Garda Reserves? What insights do you now have about the role of a Garda Trainee?

- Have you previously applied to An Garda Síochána and what were the learnings gained this time? How many Stages did you pass etc?

- Have you worked on the Diversity Internship in An Garda Síochána? What did you learn from this experience?

- Have you had work experience in a Garda Station whilst in school? Did it inspire you to apply?

So that concludes the chapter on the Application Form. My final piece of advice is to make sure you give yourself adequate time to complete it. Do not leave it to the night before the submission deadline!

If you would like to have your application form critiqued by GardaIP to ensure it maximises on your skills and abilities, reach out to us on GardaIP for more details.

Let us now get into the detail behind the Stage 1 Online Assessment.

Chapter 3

The Stage 1 Online Assessment

What is the Stage 1 Online Assessment?

The Stage 1 Online Assessment of the competition is an unsupervised assessment which you can take at home.

This assessment includes:

1. **Assessment Questionnaire**
2. **Logical Reasoning Test**
3. **Verbal Reasoning Test**

I will cover each of these in depth later in this chapter.

Candidates will be ranked based on their responses to the assessments. Those ranked highest will be invited to undertake the next stage of the selection process. Your results in the Stage 1 tests decides your placing (referred to as the Order of Merit i.e., or OOM) on the list of candidates.

As mentioned previously, if you are thinking about taking the Stage 1 Online Assessment without preparing properly to see how you go, you have missed the point about getting your best score and boosting your position on the Order of Merit.

Particularly invest time in practicing the Verbal Reasoning and Logical Reasoning Tests. Familiarity with the test type, format, and timing will significantly boost your performance on the day of the test.

Online Test-Taking Environment

Please be aware that taking these tests within a secure IT network, (for example, a network such as your work or college that might have firewalls or other security technology in place) may cause you technical difficulties. Avoid a panic meltdown! Spend time prior to taking the test to understand if this will cause an issue and undue stress for you on the day.

Therefore, I always recommend that you take the test in a familiar and comfortable environment.

Remember, the onus is on you to ensure that you have full internet access to complete the tests. My advice is to take the test at home where access to the internet is not restricted to the same level as work or college. As you know, the number of devices running on a broadband network can reduce internet speed. Therefore, reducing the number of devices connected to the internet. Run a simple broadband test in advance of taking the test too to give you a live reading of your current download speed.

In terms of devices, my advice is to take the test on a PC or laptop. Do **not** take the test on a smartphone, mobile or tablet device – you will struggle with visibility of critical information, especially when taking the Logical Reasoning Test.

Finally, you must take the assessments during the specific timeframe allocated to you. No alternative times will be granted to you by the PAS.

The Assessment Questionnaire

To assess your potential suitability for the Garda Trainee role, the assessment questionnaire collects information on your skills, interests and preferences and your responses to potential scenarios you may face in the Garda Trainee role.

The assessment questionnaire typically takes up to 60 minutes to complete. However, there is no time limit other than that you must complete and submit it within the specified assessment window. You must complete all the questions in the questionnaire.

In previous campaigns, the PAS sends you a unique assessment questionnaire link to your public jobs message board. You must then complete the test in the timeframe allocated to you.

The assessment questionnaire is split into two sections.

In **Section 1** of the assessment questionnaire, you will be given a series of statements. For some of these statements, you will be asked to indicate how well they describe you (Part A), for others you will be asked how important various characteristics are in terms of what you want from a job (Part B). The third element (Part C) asks you to rate how good you consider yourself on a range of skills compared to others you have worked or studied with.

A free, downloadable booklet is published on the Public Appointment Services (PAS) website at the start of every Garda recruitment campaign. It is called 'Notes for Candidates and Conditions of Service'. This booklet is also emailed to you by the PAS.

In this booklet there is a self-assessment questionnaire. This questionnaire is designed to gain information about you - your experience, interests, and achievements. By looking at this self-assessment questionnaire and the types of questions asked on it you can determine the qualities that are deemed necessary and relevant to the role of a Garda.

Below is a range of typical statements on the self-assessment questionnaire. Use your current and past experiences and your expectations for the future to help you decide on your response. As mentioned, there are no right and wrong answers. The response is unique to you. So be honest!

Could you:	Strongly Agree	Agree	Disagree	Strongly Disagree
Work in a role with incredible variety				
Confidently use IT packages and software				
Develop a range of new skills that you can apply in your role				
Tell a parent that their child has been killed				
Understand the complexities of relevant legislation and apply it in your role				
Perform CPR on a critically injured person				
Maintain a good level of fitness				
Enforce legislation that you personally disagree with				

Could you:	Strongly Agree	Agree	Disagree	Strongly Disagree
Arrest someone who you know to be a fundamentally honest and decent person, but who has broken the law				
Do tasks that you have been assigned that you do not particularly want to do				
Cope with large amounts of blood and other severe Injuries				
Understand that in the role you will have to deal with a huge amount of negativity, crime and, and suffering but need to maintain a positive perspective.				
Physically tackle someone resisting arrest				
Work for one organisation for your whole career				

Could you:	Strongly Agree	Agree	Disagree	Strongly Disagree
Build close working relationships with your Colleagues				
Obey a lawful order that may put you in danger				
Build strong links with a community				
Go through the possessions of a body to try to find ID				
Maintain your composure, even when severely provoked				
Be the first port of call for someone who has been sexually assaulted				
Always carry your Garda ID, even when off duty				
Build strong links with the community where you work				

Could you:	Strongly Agree	Agree	Disagree	Strongly Disagree
Work holidays including Christmas, Easter, and weekends				
Appreciate that not everyone who joins will be promoted through the ranks				
Deal with life and death situations, sometimes daily				
Adopt the shift work pattern used in An Garda Síochána, which means having to work throughout the night where, unlike some roles, sleeping is not permitted on duty				
Maintain your resilience in the face of negative coverage and unfair criticism				

Could you:	Strongly Agree	Agree	Disagree	Strongly Disagree
Appreciate that even in social situations, you are likely to be introduced to others as a Garda and some people will instantly make up their mind about you				
Carry out an arrest in a public place where you may be filmed on mobile phones				
Remain dispassionate and carry out your duties, even in very different circumstances				
Appreciate that your friends/family may worry about you and your career choice				
Go on the beat alone				
Provide help and assistance to people who need it				
Make a huge difference to the lives of others				

Assessment Questionnaire Section 2 – Job Simulation Exercise

In Section 2 you will be given several scenarios similar to what you may encounter in the role of Garda Trainee. Be aware that the Job Simulation exercise is repeated at the Stage 2 Assessment.

Before approaching section 2 (Job Simulation) it is important to understand the *typical qualities of a Garda*. Job Simulation is an exercise in putting yourself in the shoes of a member of An Garda Síochána. Therefore, do not view the role of a Garda through a narrow lens. Modern policing entails much more than crime fighting! Let me explain.

As a Garda you will work in partnership with the communities you serve to maintain law and order, protect members of the public and their property, prevent crime, reduce the fear of crime, and improve the quality of life for all members in the community you serve. You will use a range of technology to protect individuals, identify the perpetrators of crime, and ensure successful prosecutions against those who break the law.

Gardai also work closely with members of the criminal justice system, Local Authorities, social workers, schools, local businesses, the HSE, sports clubs, town planners, and community groups to provide advice, education, and assistance to those who want to reduce crime or have been affected by crime. A Garda, therefore, should have excellent interpersonal skills and the ability to work with all strands of society.

It is therefore wise to consider the following key qualities sought out in a member of An Garda Síochána. Note: these qualities will really help you in preparation for the Stage 3 Competency Interview. They are also hugely relevant for the Job Simulation exercises too – keep them at the top of your mind!

- **Effective Communication Skills** – The ability to communicate in a clear, concise, and confident manner. Points are persuasive, clearly understood, well organised, supported, and speak directly to the topic at hand.

- **Community Oriented** – The recognition and understanding of community issues and concerns. Having an insight into the role of a Garda within a community beyond law enforcement. Understanding the importance of a Garda-community partnership in identifying problems and developing solutions.

- **Interpersonal Skills** – The ability to listen to, understand, and respond effectively to others to gain information, compliance, or resolution. Perceptive and adept at understanding other's motivations and needs.

- **Respect for the Individual** – Demonstrates an understanding of, and an ability to interact and work effectively with persons of varying backgrounds, attitudes, opinions, and beliefs. Sees people as unique individuals and values their different experiences, ideas, and perspectives when solving problems.

- **Sound Judgment and Problem Solving** – Demonstrates a logical course of action based on sound reasoning. Prioritises decisions by the importance of needed actions. Considers alternatives and consequences logically.

- **Honesty and Integrity** – Demonstrates adherence to high moral and ethical principles. Possessing high ethical expectation of self and others. Willingness to assert oneself in the face of peer pressure or potential ridicule to act with honour and truthfulness. Incorruptible.

- **Teamwork** – Demonstrates the ability to successfully perform work in a team environment. Understanding of the multiple roles of team members and the importance of combined efforts.

- **Resilience** – Resolute and steady persistence in a course of action, especially despite adversity or significant difficulties. Demonstrates self-motivation and the ability to stay focused on a task despite shortcomings or limited resources.

What is the Job Simulation Exercise?

The Job Simulation test measures how you relate to a variety of Garda related scenarios (mostly Garda Trainee), which attempt to identify what you would do in a situation.

In this exercise you are presented with several scenarios similar to those you might encounter when working as a member of An Garda Síochána.

Based on previous competitions, you will have 15 minutes to respond to the eight scenarios.

For each scenario you are presented with several possible actions. You should rate each action in terms of how good or bad you think it is.

There may be scenarios where you feel all the suggested actions are good ones, or scenarios where you feel all the suggested actions are unacceptable and you would like to do something different. However, you must rate each action presented using the scale provided and based on the information in the scenario only.

The rating scale is:

1. Excellent – response meets all the needs of the situation very well.

2. Good – response meets the needs of the situation well.

3. Adequate – response is acceptable but may have some shortcomings or omissions.

4. Weak – response falls below the acceptable level.

5. Bad – response is incompetent and falls far below the acceptable level.

The easiest way to explain is to provide some typical scenarios and our suggested response along with our explanation behind the response.

You should consider each action in isolation rather than answering the question as a collective (i.e., I would first do A, then C, then B). Treat each action as an isolated action in itself.

Sample Job Simulation Exercises:

Scenario:

You've been recently assigned a new colleague. All is going very well however you have noticed that she keeps clocking out from your shifts early. This has happened 3 nights in a row. What do you do?

Rate each of following actions in isolation	Rating Scale
(A) Do nothing, just ignore it.	
(B) Inform your Sergeant and let him take over the matter.	
(C) Challenge her and ask her to explain why she is regularly leaving her shift early.	
(D) Stay calm. Choose a quiet moment on your next shift and ask her if everything is ok because you've observed that she is regularly leaving her shifts early.	

Response and Rationale:

You've been recently assigned a new colleague. All is going very well however you have noticed that she keeps clocking out from your shifts early. This has happened 3 nights in a row. What do you do?

Rate each of following actions in isolation	Rating Scale
(A) Do nothing, just ignore it.	5
(B) Inform your Sergeant and let him take over the matter.	3
(C) Challenge her and ask her to explain why she is regularly leaving her shift early.	4
(D) Stay calm. Choose a quiet moment on your next shift and ask her if everything is ok because you've observed that she is regularly leaving her shifts early.	1

- (A) is a bad response – you are choosing to ignore the issue and are taking the easy option.

- (B) is an adequate response - You are making an effort to resolve the situation. However, it is entirely possible that your colleague may have been pre-approved to leave early. Therefore, the gap here is that you should discuss the matter with her first before going to your Sergeant.

- (C) is a weak response. It is impulsive and your colleague may find your approach aggressive.

- (D) is an excellent response. There may be a very reasonable explanation for her leaving her shift early. It is always best to seek to understand first and behave rationally. It is a much more respectful approach towards your colleague.

Let us look at another one…

Scenario:

You are called to a domestic row where there is a barring order in force. On arrival you find a woman who is bleeding profusely from her head. A man is standing in the hall holding a hammer and is using threatening behaviour towards you and the woman.

Rate each of following actions in isolation	Rating Scale
A) Call a neighbour or relative to assist you	
B) Seek medical aid for the woman.	
C) Arrest the man.	
D) Send for a social worker.	
E) Leave the house as it is a private, domestic matter.	

Response and Rationale:

You are called to a domestic row where there is a Barring Order in force. On arrival you find a woman who is bleeding profusely from her head. A man is standing in the hall holding a hammer and is using threatening behaviour towards you and the woman.

Rate each of following actions in isolation	Rating Scale
A) Call a neighbour or relative to assist you	4
B) Seek medical aid for the woman.	2
C) Arrest the man.	1
D) Send for a social worker.	3
E) Leave the house as it is a private, domestic matter.	5

- (A) is a weak response – involving a neighbour or relative may escalate the issue.

- (B) is a good response – the shortcoming here, however, is that this is a violent situation where others including yourself may be in danger. Your priority is to make an arrest.

- (C) is an excellent response – you were aware in advance that a Barring Order was in force, so the man is in breach of this Order.

- (D) is an adequate response but this step comes later in the process following the taking of statements.

- (E) is a bad response – you would be leaving the aftermath of a violent episode with no guarantees that it would not escalate again.

Here is another scenario:

Scenario:

You are working at a checkpoint during Covid-19 Level 5 lockdown. You stop a car and routinely check licence and registration. The driver however is very abusive and aggressive towards you and is questioning the right of An Garda Siochana to ask him the purpose of his journey. His front seat passenger is recording this verbal exchange on his mobile phone.

Rate each of following actions in isolation	Rating Scale
(A) Explain to him that his behaviour is unacceptable and that he must cooperate.	
(B) Explain to him that her behaviour is unacceptable, request politely that he calms down, explain why the checkpoint is operational, and that if his behaviour continues you will have to arrest him for a public order offence.	
(C) Leave it to your colleague to deal with. He's very good at managing these situations with irate members of the public.	
(D) Order that the front seat passenger immediately stops recording the exchange, then deal with the drivers questions.	

Response and Rationale:

You are working at a checkpoint during Covid-19 Level 5 lockdown. You stop a car and routinely check licence and registration. The driver however is very abusive and aggressive towards you and is questioning the right of An Garda Siochana to ask him the purpose of his journey. His front seat passenger is recording this verbal exchange on his mobile phone.

Rate each of following actions in isolation	Rating Scale
(A) Explain to him that his behaviour is unacceptable and that he must cooperate.	3
(B) Explain to him that her behaviour is unacceptable, request politely that he calms down, explain why the checkpoint is operational, and that if his behaviour continues you will have to arrest him for a public order offence.	1
(C) Leave it to your colleague to deal with. He's very good at managing these situations with irate members of the public.	4
(D) Order that the front seat passenger immediately stops recording the exchange, then deal with the drivers questions.	5

- (A) is an adequate response. You are making it clear that his behaviour is unacceptable, however, the gap here is that you are not engaging with him to explain why his behaviour is unacceptable.

- (B) is an excellent response. You are calmly engaging with the driver, explaining why you are conducting the checkpoint, and explaining the implications should his behaviour continue.

- (C) is a weak response. You are passing the book here. It demonstrates poor leadership on your part.

- (D) is a bad response. There is no law against members of the public recording their dealings with An Garda Síochána. You are also not dealing with the issue at hand: which is the driver questioning the right of An Garda Siochana to ask him the purpose of his journey.

How is the Assessment Questionnaire scored?

This is a question we are frequently asked by applicants. This questionnaire is about you, your experiences, interests, and achievements. The purpose of collecting this information is to compare your preferences with characteristics that are identified as being necessary for a career in Garda Síochána in a way that is fair and consistent with everyone.

This questionnaire will be scored the same way for all applicants. The scoring system is designed to avoid discriminating against groups within the applicant population(e.g., males, females, race, ages, religion etc.).

Not all the questions count. There is no obvious way of determining which responses will attract the most points. The marks awarded are driven by preferences, with the least marks being awarded to the least preferred responses, and the most marks being awarded to the most preferred responses.

Now, let us talk in detail now about your second and third tasks in Stage 2, the Verbal Reasoning Test and Logical Reasoning Test.

The Verbal Reasoning Test:

What does the Verbal Reasoning Test involve?

The Verbal Reasoning Test is designed to evaluate how quickly and accurately you can process written information and use it to draw the correct conclusions. In short, it measures your ability to understand written information and use it to answer questions.

This tests whether you jump to conclusions, or you appreciate the limitations of a statement. You must sort fact from inference, a lot like what is required in a real work environment. It is crucial for Gardai to pass a verbal reasoning test with such an emphasis on objective, unbiased fact.

On the test, you will be presented with several short passages and asked questions on them.

Each question is a statement that you need to determine whether it is *true, false* or you *cannot say* based on the information contained in the passage.

- Select TRUE if the statement must be true based on the information in the text.

- Select FALSE if the statement is false given the information in the text.

- Select CANNOT SAY if you cannot say whether the statement is true or false without further information.

Based on previous competitions, in the actual test, you will need to complete 15 questions. The test is typically timed; however, you should be aware that there was no time limit on the test at the most recent competition.

You must complete all the questions as quickly and as accurately as you can. Although, the questions were not time limited at the last competition, your response time is recorded, and this contributes to your result.

How is the Verbal Reasoning Test marked?

The Verbal Reasoning Assessment uses Adaptive Assessment Technology. In other words, this means that you will receive questions tailored to your performance as you progress through the tests. The questions will get harder or easier based on your overall performance as you progress through the test.

Can you explain *True, False, Cannot Say*?

This is a common query from the candidates we have prepared through the years. It is easy to get bogged down in the difference between each response. Below are explanations for each.

- **TRUE.** You should only answer with 'True' if the conclusion is definitely listed in the passage. Do not make assumptions based on information that you already know outside of the passage, and do not try to draw conclusions from information that is definitely not given in the passage. For example, if the passage states that 'Mary wore a red coat to work every day' and the conclusion states that 'Mary liked wearing a red coat' this would not be TRUE, as we cannot assume that Mary wearing a red coat means she liked red coats.

- **FALSE.** You should only answer with 'False' if the conclusion is definitively not listed in the passage. Do not assume that information is false just because it is not mentioned in the passage, it can only be false is the information is disproved altogether by the passage. For example, if the passage states that 'Mary wore her red coat to work on Monday' and the conclusion states that 'Mary liked wearing her black coat to work on Mondays' this would not be FALSE, as we cannot assume that Mary did not like wearing her black coat on Mondays.

- **CANNOT SAY.** You should only answer with 'Cannot Say' if the conclusion is not listed in the passage. If there is no way to definitively answer with True or False, then you should answer with 'Cannot Say'. For example, if the passage states that 'Mary wore a red coat because she liked the colour' and the conclusion states that 'Red was Mary's favourite colour' then the answer would be CANNOT SAY, as there is no way for us to ascertain whether red was Mary's favourite colour.

One of the most common pitfalls that derails candidates is using outside knowledge! To avoid this, you should base your reasoning on the assumption that factual statements in the passages are true for the sake of this test, even if you believe them to be false in the real world. In other words, leave your own knowledge at the door! You must base your answer only from the information that is provided in each passage.

Do I need to be a fast reader?

It helps, but what is more important than speed is how well you understand what you are reading and recognising the difference between fact and inference. You will need to strike a balance between attempting lots of questions and getting correct what you have attempted.

What is the best technique for the Verbal Reasoning Test?

Through practice you will develop your own technique to the best of your ability. However, there is a general technique that we always recommend that candidates follow.

1. Read the entire passage through once, then turn to the questions in-turn.

2. Read the first statement and refer to the relevant part of the passage to carefully consider if the statement is true, false, or impossible to determine (Cannot Say) without further information.

3. It will often come down to just one or two sentences within the passage.

4. During your test have an idea of how much time to allow yourself for each question and know when to move on.

5. Do not guess. Beware some tests do have mechanisms for detecting random guessing, and this won't look good when the PAS Assessor sees that you are an impulsive risk taker. So, do not be tempted to guess the questions!

6. Base your answers on only the information contained in the passage. This is crucial and if you do not do this you will probably get a lot of the questions wrong. Verbal reasoning tests are not testing what you know, they are testing how well you understand written information.

Verbal Reasoning Sample Questions and Answers

Example 1:

If you are trying to lose weight, skipping meals may not be a prudent option. Some people often go on a 'diet' by skipping lunch or dinner altogether. Their logic seems simple. If you are not eating, you are holding back on calorie intake. As a result, weight gain is arrested. However, modern studies have, time and again, refuted this claim. Skipping meals may, in fact, trigger what experts call an 'evolutionary response to famine'. Your body tries to conserve energy by slowing down metabolism and storing up on fat. So, instead of skipping meals, it is more advisable to eat regularly, eat in moderation, and intake fewer calories. Spend time in physical activities to burn those extra calories instead. Do not starve.

Physical activities are better alternatives to skipping meals.

A. True

B. False

C. Cannot Say

Answer: A True

The last two lines state that – 'Spend time in physical activities to burn those extra calories instead. Do not starve.'

Example 2:

If you are trying to lose weight, skipping meals may not be a prudent option. Some people often go on a 'diet' by skipping lunch or dinner altogether. Their logic seems simple. If you are not eating, you are holding back on calorie intake. As a result, weight gain is arrested. However, modern studies have, time and again, refuted this claim. Skipping meals may, in fact, trigger what experts call an 'evolutionary response to famine'. Your body tries to conserve energy by slowing down metabolism and storing up on fat. So, instead of skipping meals, it is more advisable to eat regularly, eat in moderation and intake fewer calories. Spend time in physical activities to burn those extra calories instead. Do not starve.

The logic behind giving up regular meals is simple and attested by modern studies.

A. True

B. False

C. Cannot Say

Answer: B False

The paragraph states that modern studies have 'refuted this claim'.

Example 3:

Strawberries are often underrated as source of nutrients in our daily diet. They are not only delicious, but are also rich in antioxidants, vitamins, fibres and essential minerals like manganese and potassium. As a source of vitamin C, strawberries are said to be comparable to oranges in reducing risk of chronic diseases and lowering high blood pressure. Though often used in desserts, strawberries are low in sugar and calorie content. In medieval days, they were treasured for perceived aphrodisiac properties. While picking your strawberries from shop shelves, check out for the fresh ones – the ones that are dark red, dotted with yellow seeds on the surface and with dark green leafy caps that are not wilted.

Despite being underappreciated, strawberries are rich in essential nutrients.

A. True

B. False

C. Cannot Say

Answer: A True

As per the passage, strawberries are rich in nutrients necessary for a healthy diet.

Example 4:

Strawberries are often underrated as source of nutrients in our daily diet. They are not only delicious, but are also rich in antioxidants, vitamins, fibres and essential minerals like manganese and potassium. As a source of vitamin C, strawberries are said to be comparable to oranges in reducing risk of chronic diseases and lowering high blood pressure. Though often used in desserts, strawberries are low in sugar and calorie content. In medieval days, they were treasured for perceived aphrodisiac properties. While picking your strawberries from shop shelves, check out for the fresh ones – the ones that are dark red, dotted with yellow seeds on the surface and with dark green leafy caps that are not wilted.

Locally produced strawberries procured from the farmers' market taste better than frozen ones.

A. True

B. False

C. Cannot Say

Answer: C, Cannot Say

Even if our personal experiences can prove or disprove otherwise, there is nothing in the given passage that can definitely mark this inference as either true or false.

The Logical Reasoning Test

What does the Logical Reasoning Test involve?

The Logical Reasoning Test is designed to test your problem-solving ability. It identifies your ability to breakdown information in order to answer questions on the abstract patterns presented. You are tested on whether you can analyse the visual graphics displayed and to logically deduce the correct answer based on the answer options.

The test typically contains 15 questions, but this can vary from competition to competition.

The objective is to complete all the questions as quickly and as accurately as you can. Although each question is not time limited, as per the Verbal Reasoning Test, your response time is recorded and will contribute to your result.

In the test, you are presented with various abstract patterns, arranged in sequence. You will need to predict the next item in the sequence – following the same underlying pattern. Your task is to select the correct answer from the options provided.

What are the types of Logical Reasoning Tests you should prepare for?

The PAS have, on occasion, changed the format of the Logical Reasoning Test.

Specifically, there are 3 test types you need to familiar with:

1. 'Find the Next in Series'

2. 'Find the Odd One Out'

3. 'Abstract Reasoning'

The best and easiest way for me to explain each type of test is by providing examples with answers.

Let me first set out the most frequently occurring patterns in Logical Reasoning.

The Frequently Occurring Patterns

The most frequently occurring patterns are:

1. Change of figures along the quadrants of the holding square frame.

2. Movement of figures along the perimeter of the holding square frame

   • Linear movement of figures inside the frame

   • Circular movement of figures inside the frame

   • Clockwise movement, anticlockwise movement, and in place rotation

3. Sequences and set patterns within and across frames.

Logical Reasoning Test Type 1: Find the Next in Series

This test, 'Find the Next in Series' is the one most widely used by the PAS. It was last used for Garda Entry Assessment in 2018.

In this test you are presented with five boxes, which are arranged in a logical sequence. Your task is to select the box, which you believe, comes next in the sequence.

To select your answer, please choose one of the boxes marked A to E. As promised above, the best and easiest way to explain this test type is by providing examples and explanations.

Example 1 – Find the Next in Series

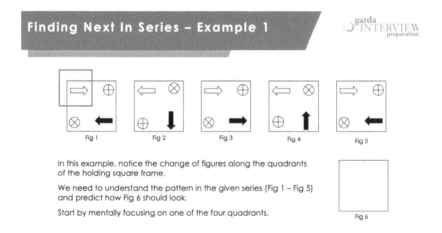

Finding Next In Series – Example 1

garda INTERVIEW preparation

Fig 1   Fig 2   Fig 3   Fig 4   Fig 5

In this example, notice the change of figures along the quadrants of the holding square frame.

We need to understand the pattern in the given series (Fig 1 – Fig 5) and predict how Fig 6 should look.

Start by mentally focusing on one of the four quadrants.

Fig 6

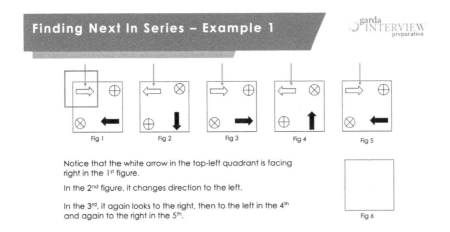

Finding Next In Series – Example 1

Fig 1   Fig 2   Fig 3   Fig 4   Fig 5

Fig 6

Notice that the white arrow in the top-left quadrant is facing right in the 1st figure.

In the 2nd figure, it changes direction to the left.

In the 3rd, it again looks to the right, then to the left in the 4th and again to the right in the 5th.

www.gardaip.com

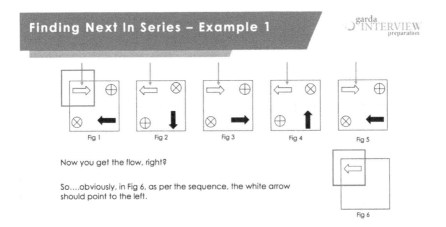

Finding Next In Series – Example 1

Fig 1   Fig 2   Fig 3   Fig 4   Fig 5

Fig 6

Now you get the flow, right?

So....obviously, in Fig 6, as per the sequence, the white arrow should point to the left.

www.gardaip.com

Finding Next In Series – Example 1

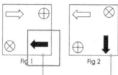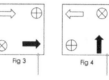

Fig 1   Fig 2   Fig 3   Fig 4   Fig 5

Fig 6

Moving on to the bottom-right quadrant, notice that the direction of the black arrow changes. But is there a pattern?

In the 1st figure, the arrow faces left.

In the 2nd figure, the arrow faces down.

In the 3rd figure, the arrow faces right.

In the 4th figure, the arrow faces up.

In the 5th figure, the arrow faces left again.

Finding Next In Series – Example 1

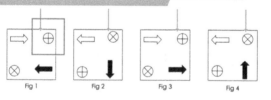

Fig 1   Fig 2   Fig 3   Fig 4   Fig 5

Fig 6

Next, move on to the top-right quadrant.

Notice that the crossed circle changes from one with a '+' sign in the middle to one with an 'x' in the middle.

And the sequence repeats.

So...going by the sequence '+', 'x', '+', 'x', '+', the Fig 6 should have a circle with an 'x' in the top-right quadrant.

Finding Next In Series – Example 1

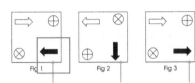 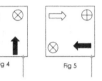

So, what will be the direction of the black arrow in the next figure?

Guessed it right…..it should face down again!

Finding Next In Series – Example 1

  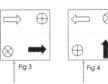

That leaves us only with the bottom-left quadrant.

Similar to what we saw for the top-right corner, the sequence is

'circle with x' → circle with +' → 'circle with x' → circle with +' → 'circle with x' .

So the Fig 6 should have a 'circle with +' in the bottom left corner.

That's it!

Example 2 – Find the Next in Series

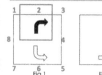

Fig 1   Fig 2   Fig 3   Fig 4   Fig 5

In this example, notice the use of clockwise movement and in place rotation of figures.

It is evident that both the black and white arrows rotate, and the black arrow additionally changes positions in each frame.

Let us start with the black arrow.

Trick is to mentally make a map of the path the moving figure takes and predict the next step.

Think of a circular path for the figure touching the corners of the square frame and the middle of each side.

Fig 6

Finding Next In Series – Example 2

Fig 1   Fig 2   Fig 3   Fig 4   Fig 6

Now notice that the black arrow also rotates as it moves along the perimeter of the square.

It is apparent that at each step it rotates 90 degrees to the right.

So, keeping with the pattern, in position 7 of Fig 6, it will start from top-left and point towards bottom-right as shown.

Fig 6

Test Type 2 – 'Find the Odd One Out'

This format, called 'Find the Odd One Out' was last used in the 2016 Garda Entry competition.

Your task is to mark the object out of a row of objects that does not fit the rule of the other objects. Each row consists of objects of which exactly one is wrong and has to be discovered.

Example 1 – Find the Odd One Out

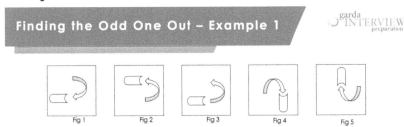

Finding the Odd One Out – Example 1

garda INTERVIEW preparation

Fig 1   Fig 2   Fig 3   Fig 4   Fig 5

Welcome to the 1st example of 'Finding The Odd One Out' type of questions!

The general trick is to focus on each item in one set and check primarily 3 cases:

1. If it has changed in any ONE of the other figures (that's the odd one out!)

2. If it has changed across the figures in any specific pattern – alone, as part of a group, or in relation to any other item
    ✓ if so, does the pattern break in any ONE of the other figures (that's the odd one out!)

3. If it has changed in any of the other figures, but there is no obvious pattern then simply ignore it and move to the next item

Repeat for the next item in the same set one by one till you **zone in on the odd one out.**   www.gardaip.com

Finding the Odd One Out – Example 1

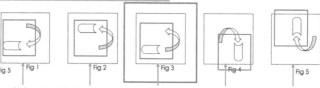

Fig 5   Fig 1   Fig 2   Fig 3   Fig 4   Fig 5

Start by focusing on Fig 1.

That's generally a good place to start.

Move across the figures from left to right and see if an item has changed - alone, as part of a group, or in relation to any other item.

Do you notice the odd one? Look at Fig 3.

In all other frames the curved arrow is pointing towards the concave face of the other figure.

In this, the curved arrow is facing away.

Congratulations! You got the Odd One Out!

Example 2 – Find the Odd One Out

Finding the Odd One Out – Example 2

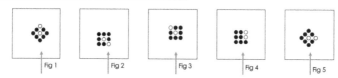

Fig 1   Fig 2   Fig 3   Fig 4   Fig 5

Let us consider another type – an item or an aggregate of items rotates about itself or around the perimeter of the square frame.

Trick is to keep an eye on the rotation and spot the pattern and identify the figure where it breaks.

Consider the group of dots as a single composite item. Trace it through the figures from left to right.

Finding the Odd One Out – Example 2

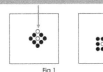
Fig 1

Fig 2

Fig 3

Fig 4

Fig 5

Fig 1: The composite figure has 2 dots that are white – one in the corner and the other in the centre.

Fig 2: The group is rotated – the set of white dots now points to the bottom-right corner.

Fig 3: The group is rotated – the set of white dots now points to the top-left corner.

Fig 4: The group is rotated – the set of white dots now change positions: there is no longer a white dot in the centre and one dot in the side has turned white instead.

No need to check Fig 5 now – **Fig 4 is the Odd One Out!**

www.gardaip.com

Test Type 3 – Abstract Reasoning

'Abstract Reasoning' is another Logical Reasoning Test type used by the PAS.

Your task is to identify a pattern within the series and decide what you think should replace the missing box choosing from the answer options available.

Example 1 – Abstract Reasoning

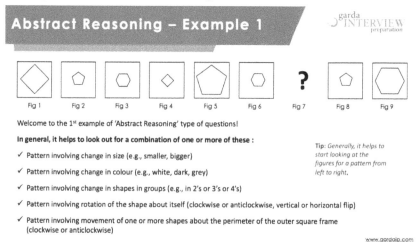

Abstract Reasoning – Example 1

garda INTERVIEW preparation

Fig 1 Fig 2 Fig 3 Fig 4 Fig 5 Fig 6 Fig 7 Fig 8 Fig 9

Welcome to the 1st example of 'Abstract Reasoning' type of questions!

In general, it helps to look out for a combination of one or more of these :

✓ Pattern involving change in size (e.g., smaller, bigger)

✓ Pattern involving change in colour (e.g., white, dark, grey)

✓ Pattern involving change in shapes in groups (e.g., in 2's or 3's or 4's)

✓ Pattern involving rotation of the shape about itself (clockwise or anticlockwise, vertical or horizontal flip)

✓ Pattern involving movement of one or more shapes about the perimeter of the outer square frame (clockwise or anticlockwise)

Tip: Generally, it helps to start looking at the figures for a pattern from left to right.

www.gardaip.com

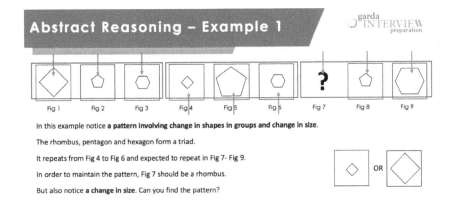

Abstract Reasoning – Example 1

In this example notice **a pattern involving change in shapes in groups and change in size**.

The rhombus, pentagon and hexagon form a triad.

It repeats from Fig 4 to Fig 6 and expected to repeat in Fig 7- Fig 9.

In order to maintain the pattern, Fig 7 should be a rhombus.

But also notice **a change in size**. Can you find the pattern?

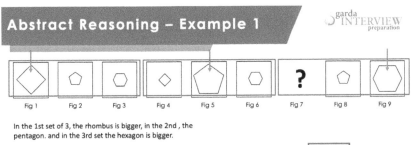

Abstract Reasoning – Example 1

In the 1st set of 3, the rhombus is bigger, in the 2nd , the pentagon. and in the 3rd set the hexagon is bigger.

That means, in the 3rd triad (Fig 7 to Fig 9), the rhombus is NOT bigger in shape.

So, the shape enclosed in Fig 7 would be a small rhombus. That's your answer!

Abstract Reasoning – Example 1

That gives you the final figure that fits nicely into the pattern!

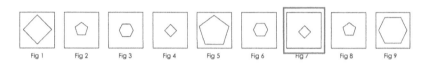

Example 2 – Abstract Reasoning

Abstract Reasoning – Example 2

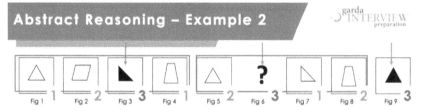

Notice, the colour of the shape changes to black in positions 3 and 9.

So, if the shape is black in position 6 – we get a repeating pattern:
The shapes repeat in sets of 4 and the shape turns black in every 3rd figure.

Thus, the shape enclosed in Fig 6 would be a black parallelogram.

Abstract Reasoning – Example 2

In this example notice **a pattern involving change in shapes in group and change in colour**.

The equilateral triangle, parallelogram, right-angle triangle and trapezoid form a set from Fig 1 to Fig 4.

Expectedly, 3 out of 4 of these shapes repeat in order from Fig 5 to Fig 8.

Also, the 9th figure, Fig 9, starts as expected – with a triangle, vetting our assumption.

In order to maintain the pattern, Fig 6 should be a parallelogram.

But also notice **a change in colour**. Can you find the pattern?

Abstract Reasoning – Example 2

That gives you the final figure that fits nicely into the pattern!

Tip: *Sometimes it also helps to check the given answer options and work backwards.*
You use the method of elimination to arrive at the missing figure. But both ways, the logic to deduce the answer would be the same.
Use whatever is convenient to you.

Our Top Tips for Logical Reasoning

Tip 1: Keep it Simple

Logical Reasoning questions will require you to find the most simple and logical answer. It may feel like the questions are out to trick you, and that may lead to you trialling overly complex rules.

However, in many situations, the simple pattern is the correct pattern. For example, if you have a question with several elements, find the element where you can see a simple pattern. This can give you an answer that you can then check with the other elements.

Tip 2: Build your Patterns

One cannot see what the mind does not know! Therefore, it is important to be familiar with as many patterns as you can, through practice. The patterns in these tests will become very familiar to you over time. From this pattern database, you can build a general approach to each type of question.

Tip 3: Learn Strategies

There are various strategies that can be used to solve Logical Reasoning questions quickly. One technique is mapping, which can be particularly useful in the early stages of your preparation(i.e., isolate each element and then figure out the rules).

Tip 4: Practice

Ultimately, nothing beats Practice! The more Logical Reasoning questions you attempt, the faster and more accurate you will become. See our Appendix on where to purchase these Tests.

If you need additional support for the Stage 1 Assessment, our online tutorials at GardaIP.com will prepare you with total confidence to be ready to take the Assessment Questionaire and Garda aptitude tests (Verbal and logical reasoning).

Chapter 4

The Stage 2 Assessment

What is the Stage 2 Assessment?

The Stage 2 Assessment is a repeat of the Stage 1 in a supervised environment along with two additional tests. The Assessment typically takes place at the PAS Offices in Middle Abbey Street, Dublin. However, this may change in our new post-Covid world.

Stage 2 is made up of the following assessments:

1. Re-test of the two Aptitude Tests undertaken in the first stage i.e.,

   a. Verbal Reasoning and

   b. Logical Reasoning

2. Job Simulation Exercises

3. Report Writing Exercise

The test is conducted in supervised conditions to ensure that candidates did not cheat when attempting the Stage1 online assessments without supervision!

If your performance on these supervised re-tests is outside the expected scoring range of your Stage 1 unsupervised test result, you may be excluded from subsequent stages of the selection process.

The failure rate in these tests is high. Your results in these tests decides your placing on the list of candidates and dictates where you are placed in the Order of Merit. The higher you score, the faster the turnaround in time to your Stage 3 Competency Interview.

1. Supervised Re-tests (of previously taken Verbal and Logical Reasoning Tests)

All candidates invited to the Assessment Centre are re-tested on the Verbal Reasoning Test and Logical Reasoning Test. These tests are conducted on-line in PAS's computer test-suite.

These tests are of similar nature to the tests you took online at Stage 1 of the selection process.

Therefore, there is no need to cover these tests again – please refer to Chapter 3 instead.

2. Job Simulation Exercise

This exercise is a repeat of the job simulation exercise you completed at Stage 1.

In this exercise you are presented with several scenarios similar to those you might encounter when working as a member of An Garda Síochána.

Typically you will have 15 minutes for the 8 scenarios, with four to five responses for each scenario.

For each scenario you are presented with several possible actions. You should rate each action in terms of how good or bad you think it is.

We covered the Job Simulation Exercise in detail in Chapter 3.

3. The Report Writing Exercise

Why is Report Writing so Important to An Garda Síochána?

Report writing is a central duty in the life of a Garda. Think about it. If you are a Garda attending the scene of an incident, the write up should be an accurate and detailed report outlining what happened, which can be central to any investigations or inquiries which follow.

As part of a Garda's duties, they are required to write descriptions of incidents which they encounter. These incidents could be a road traffic accident, an aggravated assault, a case of domestic violence, a burglary etc. These descriptions are especially important as they are submitted to the Garda's supervisor and are frequently used in court cases. Therefore, it is important that these descriptions accurately reflect the information obtained.

Even when there is no investigation involved, reports may be required to apply for promotion, transfer, or to deliver information up through the levels of management in the organisation. Gardai must ensure that their reports are accurate, detailed, and objective.

How does the Report Writing Exercise work on the day of the Test?

Before you begin to write your report, you will first watch a video which will be shown on a large screen in the test-suite. There will be lots of information communicated on the video and your role is to write a report based on what you have seen and heard.

You may take notes during the video which you can then use when writing your report. I will give you tips on note taking further on in the chapter.

The instructions for the exercise will also be communicated at the start of the video, so it is important to pay full attention from the very beginning.

During this exercise you are to assume that you are a Garda arriving with a colleague at a scene where an incident has taken place. Assume that you are the Garda asking questions and that the camera is your eyes and ears.

After you have viewed the scene, you will be given exactly 30 minutes to complete a written report summarising the incident. This provides a measure of your ability to produce a concise and accurate description of what you have seen and heard.

The Report Writing Marking Scheme

Your written communication skills are measured by the Report Writing exercise.

In this exercise you will be assessed on the following:

1. Accuracy of content

2. Literacy and structure (e.g., spelling/ language/ grammar/ punctuation)

You must reach the required standard on each of these elements in order to qualify at this exercise. Marks will be deducted for errors and exaggerations, or false information not provided in the video.

Let us get into the detail on accuracy, literacy, and structure of the report.

Accuracy of Content

In terms of 'accuracy', it is important that the information you put in your report is correct and comprehensive. The facts you hear should be communicated as facts; you will be penalised for including information based on your own assumptions or information not included in the video.

There is critical information that will always feature; therefore, be prepared to take notes on.

- Names
- Addresses
- Dates of birth
- Contact numbers (mobile)
- Car registration numbers

So, play smart. You know that this critical detail will need to be recorded on the day of the test, therefore prepare your roughwork notes in advance to capture this information.

Literacy and Structure:

The second area of the Marking Scheme is 'literacy and structure'. Let us deal with literacy first.

Literacy:

The report should be written in formal plain English; it is not acceptable to use slang or "text speak" in this report. The grammar used in the report should be correct; the tenses used should be consistent. We always recommend writing the report in the past tense. It is important that the report is written fluently; it must be easy to read, makes sense, and flows well.

Pay close attention to spelling, however, marks will not be deducted where a reasonable attempt has been made to spell names and places correctly.

The information in your report should be clear and well laid out. You must complete your report in the time allowed, which is typically 30 minutes.

So that is literacy. What about structure?

Structure:

The structure of the Report is very important. The Garda must describe everything that he observed at the scene. Victims are identified, perpetrators are described based upon witness testimony, the scene (time and place) is recorded, and the situation is summarised.

The good news is that the structure of the report that we recommend is very easy to remember!

The description must consist of facts – what you (the Garda) saw, heard, observed, and experienced.

Follow this Structure:

1st Paragraph: Set the Scene

1. Date, time, and location

2. State your name and rank

3. Additional Gardai – state their name and their rank

4. Why were you at the scene?

5. How you arrived (e.g., Car, Foot, Bike etc.)?

6. Nature of the call or incident (e.g., burglary, assault, car accident)

7. Location of the call or incident

2nd Paragraph / 3rd paragraph / 4th paragraph: Witness Statements

– Witness 1: This is where you give a summary of the witness statement. Give details of:

- Name
- Address
- Date of Birth
- Phone Number
- Then provide his/her full account of the incident. This part of the report should be as rich as possible. Be as thorough as you can and remember to include as many details as necessary for that particular report.

– Repeat for Witness 2 / Witness 3 etc

Note: Typically, on the day of the test there are only two Witnesses.

Use our Checklist to ensure you have captured the critical detail in your Report:

- Your report clearly states the crime/event that occurred.

- Your report identifies the scene (time and place).

- Your report summarises the crime/event in chronological order (beginning, middle, end).

- Your report includes details about what was seen / heard by each witness.

- Your report is factual (i.e., it is objective).

- Your report is structured in paragraphs rather than one long paragraph.

- Your report contains correct spelling.

- Your report contains correct punctuation and grammar.

Do not Forget to complete the General Questions Form!

This is a short exercise that examines your listening skills. Once the video has finished you will have 30 minutes to write your report and you will also have to complete some general questions during this time.

These are basic questions that you will have captured in your rough notes such as witness 1 name, address, phone number, date of birth, car registration etc.

My 4 Big Tips for Report Writing

1. You do not need to watch the video. Keep your head down, listen, and write. Looking up will distract you and you may not capture all the information you need.

2. You need to be prepared to hear strong accents on the video. In previous campaigns candidates have struggled to tune their ear to a strong Dublin accent, Cork accent, Eastern European accent etc. Adjust your ear by listening to local radio stations, watching soaps on TV, and downloading podcasts.

3. You will be assessed on the content of your description of the situation represented in the video (i.e., on your ability to distinguish between facts, non-factual information, and irrelevant information). Use only the information in the video and do not invent information yourself. Remember it is always facts over feelings!

4. Practice, practice, practice. I cannot emphasise enough the need to adequately prepare for this test. See our appendix on where you can purchase a Stage 2 Preparation Course that includes Report Writing exercises and model reports.

If you need additional support to get ready to sit the Garda Aptitude Tests, Job Simulation Exercises and Report Writing, check out the online tutorials at GardaIP to get exam ready.

Chapter 5

The Stage 3 Competency Interview

Introduction

After successfully passing Stage 2, it is time for the challenging part. More than 80 percent of the initial applicants have already been eliminated. This is where the real work begins.

Let us peel everything back and pause for one minute while I explain the simplicity of an Interview.

The interview panel are seeking the answers to three fundamental questions.

1. **Can you do the job of a Garda?** *Can you provide evidence that your experience matches the qualities (competencies) of a Garda (e.g., qualifications etc)?*

2. **Will you do the job of a Garda well?** *Are you self-motivated, can you work independently, will you put effort in to making it a success?*

3. **Are you a good fit for An Garda Síochána?** *Are you passionate about a career in An Garda Síochána and are your values in line with those of the organisation? Are you a team player? Can you follow instruction? Do you respect authority?*

All levels of An Garda Síochana now use competency-based interviews. From potential new recruits to serving Gardaí who want to apply for specialist units or internal promotion. Everyone must master competency-based interview techniques as they are used all across the Garda organisation, from entry level to lateral appointments and promotions.

We are often asked what is competency-based selection? The most simple explanation is competency based interviewing is a structured interview technique based on the assumption that past behaviour predicts future behaviour.

What is the Garda Trainee Stage 3 Competency Interview?

Stage 3 is a formal competency based interview. The competencies are key skills deemed necessary to serve effectively as a member of An Garda Síochána.

The interview with the 3-person Board typically lasts 45 minutes and takes place at the PAS head office in Dublin. This face-to-face format may change in our new post-Covid world, however.

The majority of your interview will focus on an examination of five core competencies (and may be subject to change by the PAS).

The five competencies are:

1. Exercising Authority

2. Resilience

3. Conscientiousness

4. Interpersonal Skills and Service Ethos

5. Using Information and Problem Solving

During the interview you are asked to give examples of instances when you displayed each of the competencies effectively. Specific examples will be explored by the interview panel in depth. You must provide full details and explain the context of the situation, the actions you took, the behaviours you demonstrated, and your contribution to the outcome.

Most people pick examples from their previous work experience, voluntary experience, educational experience, or a hobby that they enjoy.

The panel will ask follow up questions for further clarification, particularly in relation to your specific actions and behaviours.

Before the Interview

The interview is the first opportunity An Garda Síochána has to meet you. Therefore, you want to make a good impression. Your goal is to convince them that you possess the qualities of a good Garda.

Before you even enter the interview room, there are several things you will want to consider in preparation for the competency interview.

The Application Form

As discussed in great depth in Chapter 2, when applying for An Garda Síochána the Application Form must be submitted first – essentially this is your CV. I cannot emphasise the importance of putting time and effort into populating this form enough – fill out each section and ensure it is spell checked before you submit it.

The panel will be reviewing the information you have included on your Application Form. If there are uncompleted portions or you are missing certain detail, this may reflect poorly on you. It gives the interviewers insight into your organisational and communication abilities.

Be prepared to discuss every detail on your Application Form. It is your form, so it is important to be familiar with it. A good Application Form can help steer the interviewers' questions in the direction you are most comfortable with.

Looking Your Best

It is a given that most interviewers will expect a man to wear a suit and tie, and a woman to wear business attire to the interview.

You may look good wearing nice casual slacks, but you will look even better to the Panel if you wear business attire. You want to project a professional image. As you enter the interviewing room, greet everyone with a firm handshake. Look them in the eye and smile as you greet them. Remember, you are applying for a law enforcement position. This is a field in which you have to deal with people. You want to show the panel that you are a confident person. Giving someone a weak handshake while looking away is a poor way to commence an interview!

What to expect on the day

In the weeks prior to the interview, you should carefully review the five competencies and start matching your experience and accomplishments against the requirements of each. You do not want to go into the interview winging it. Everyone is nervous to some extent when sitting in front of an interview panel. You want to look and sound your best. Avoid becoming tongue-tied by rehearsing your answers. Do a mock interview with a family member or a friend.

Your interview will be approximately 45 minutes in length. You will be questioned by a panel of three people. They will be seated on one side of a table. On the other side of the table will be your chair. In most cases, your chair will be approximately six to ten feet away from the table. In this set up, the interviewers want you to sit a short distance away from them. This allows them to see your entire body and observe your mannerisms.

You should answer all of the questions truthfully. If you pass the interview, An Garda Síochána will conduct a background investigation. If, during their investigation, they discover that you were less than truthful about the smallest of things, you will be disqualified. You are applying for a position in which you must uphold the law. Therefore, they are looking for integrity.

Most people are a little nervous during the interview. This is a very normal response. To help you relax, pause before answering a question. Take a brief moment to think about your answer before responding. Take a sip of water and use this time to reflect on the question. This will help you to collect your thoughts.

As you answer the questions, speak clearly and loudly. Oral communication is key to a career in An Garda Síochána. One moment you may be chatting with the public and the next moment you may be giving forceful verbal commands to a suspect. The panel is assessing your ability to communicate by what you say and how you say it. Speaking in a low tone of voice is not what they want to hear--meek and mild are not the traits of a good Garda. You only get one chance to make a first impression.

The panel will be writing throughout the interview. Do not let this bother you. Just because they are writing something down does not mean it is a negative comment. They may be noting your good qualities, or simply going through a checklist. You should be more concerned if they do not take any notes! Be prepared to see a fourth person in the room – a note taker will be present too and will not ask you any questions.

The interview panel is not out to get you! The role of the panel is to simply help select the right candidate. Remember, the interview is a two-way discussion where the panel wants you to perform well.

The interview panel will not ask you any questions concerning the law or their specific policies and procedures. You will be taught all of that at the Garda College Templemore. They will usually begin the interview by verifying the information you provided to them in your Application Form – they will quickly review your academic, work and voluntary achievements. Then, they will then begin to probe into the competencies in great detail.

Let us now cover each of the competencies in greater detail.

Core Competencies for An Garda Síochána

The interview panel will be looking for specific and relevant examples under the following competencies (and may be subject to change by the PAS). The official description under each competency is set out below.

Interpersonal Skills and Service Ethos: *[handwritten: Elderly / foreign / illiterate. / Relationships with cust.]*

Is motivated to serve others / the public, is helpful and engages with others in a positive and constructive way that facilitates relationship building, underpinned by respect and a sensitivity to other's needs. Possesses sound social skills such as sensitivity to the situation, the ability to listen and understand a range of perspectives and needs and respond with appropriate language and actions. *[handwritten: loss /will. dept /stuck for money.]*

Exercising Authority: *[handwritten: taking control]*

Demonstrates the ability and willingness to take a clear and credible lead, having the self-assurance to make rapid, well-judged, and potentially unpopular decisions, executing and standing by them.

Conscientiousness: *[handwritten: Punctual. hard working]*

Operates diligently, honourably, and proactively, getting work done to the required standards and putting in effort. Demonstrates professionalism and persistence, being motivated to do the right thing and seeing tasks through to the end, despite adversity.

everyday work   *Leaving Cert*

Resilience:

The ability to cope with a demanding workload and to deal calmly and objectively with difficult situations, crises, and trauma. Demonstrates a desire for continual learning and self-development, seeking and accepting feedback from others.   *AIB*

Using Information and Problem Solving:

Time for calls

Foreign – no english.   *Elderly woman / speak privately*

Suspicious Transaction Demonstrates strong problem-solving skills with an ability to effectively assimilate and evaluate information from a range of sources to support good quality decision-making and generate solutions that meet the needs of a given situation or wider objective.

My advice is to list all these competencies and then think of several examples for each. These examples should show how you behaved in a way that demonstrates the competency being examined. Typically, your examples will come from three areas: your work, your college studies, and your extracurricular activities. The more examples, the better, as you are going to whittle them down.

Now, narrow down the examples to two really good, compelling ones for each competency. You will need two well prepared examples for the actual interview.

Structuring your Examples

You must deliver your answers in an organised way. A competency interview is storytelling with a start, middle, and happy ending. Much like good storytellers, it is important to paint a complete picture of the scenario for the panel and then to make an impact with your actions taken and the outcome achieved.

Structure your examples in a way that makes it easy for you to discuss and most importantly easy for the Interview Panel to evaluate.

Use the **STAR** structure.

- Situation
- Task
- Action
- Result

Situation: Describe the situation that you were in at the time. Keep it brief – what problem or situation were you faced with that you had to overcome?

Task: What was your task or objective? What did you have to do? This should be one or two sentences at most. It needs to be focused.

Action: Explain what you did / how you did it / why you did it. The panel will expect you to expand on your actions. By this I mean you must explain what you did and why you did it.

Result: Explain what happened– how it all ended. Also, use the opportunity to describe what you accomplished and what you learned in that situation.

Preparing Your Examples

Ensure your examples are concise – do not ramble off course. Make sure that each example has a noticeably clear connection to the competency you want to demonstrate, and make sure you use your own words – it should flow naturally with practice.

Make sure that your examples are about you-- in terms of showing you in the best possible light. You are front and centre – you are the person that contributed to the scenario rather than observing or being on the periphery of the situation. In other words, the example cannot be about you playing a minor part.

With that in mind, please ensure that you are comfortable talking about 'me, myself, and I'. This is the most common failing I observed at the interview stage. Most of us are modest and like to play down our positive contribution to situations. However, in a competency interview the board are looking for evidence of where, what, why, and how **you** uniquely contributed to the situation.

Finally, make sure your examples deal with concrete facts. In other words, the example must be based on past experiences. It will become quite obvious to the interview panel if the example is made up or not based on your experiences.

The secret to success at the Competency Interview is to truly understand how each competency relates to the Garda Trainee role. Then, you demonstrate how you can match the demands of the Garda Trainee role with your experience.

Be prepared for Probing!

Sometimes a member of the interview panel will up the ante and play 'bad cop'. This typically involves putting pressure on you to see how you react to pressure. It is a tactic to get a steer on your temperament.

Some interviewers like to bombard candidates with probes which may make you feel uncomfortable or even under attack! The most important thing to remember here is to not take the tone and approach personally and to focus on the question. I always tell candidates to imagine the questions as a tennis ball that you must play back to the other side of the court whilst always keeping the ball within the lines. Play the ball, not the man!

Probes are best explained by example. If the main question is "Tell us about a time you experienced working as part of a team". Further probes could be:

- Who else was on your team?

- What were you trying to achieve as a team?

- What role did you play on the team?

- You said that somebody was not pulling their weight on the team, what did you do about it?

The difference between making a statement and backing that statement up.

This is hugely important. I cannot emphasise this enough. Do not make a statement about yourself without backing it up with an example. Always volunteer information to support your answer. Let me explain.

"I am a fantastic team player. I have been playing football at senior level for the past seven years."

The above is simply a statement.

You need to talk about the role you play on the team, the role that others play, and how you all work toward success each season. What have you learned about yourself as a team player? How would your teammates describe you? I could go on and on!

Ok, so now let us cover each competency in more depth and understand why they are being examined by the interview panel.

Interpersonal Skills and Service Ethos:

Here is the official description of the competency:

Is motivated to serve others / the public, is helpful and engages with others in a positive and constructive way that facilitates relationship building, underpinned by respect and a sensitivity to others' needs. Possesses sound social skills such as sensitivity to the situation, the ability to listen and understand a range of perspectives and needs and responds with appropriate language and actions.

Why are Interpersonal Skills and Service Ethos important to the role of a Garda Trainee?

The panel is looking for evidence that you are warm and approachable and can build strong relationships with others inside and outside of your place of work.

Once you become a Garda you will need to be effective at working with others, and I do not just mean working with your colleagues. A Garda must have a strong commitment to good public service. This is especially important because the central aim of An Garda Síochána is to work in the interests of public safety and welfare.

To meet this aim, it is essential that a Garda believes in and can provide a high level of service. Good public service means that you are responsible, polite, and considerate at all times. By utilising these traits, Gardaí can earn the trust of the public and enhance the reputation of An Garda Síochána. If you have experience dealing directly with the public, then this provides you with an excellent opportunity to demonstrate your commitment to the highest levels of customer service. Have you worked in retail, foodservice, hospitality, or in any job where you are dealing with the public every day?

As a Garda you will also have to communicate and work with other stakeholders and organisations too, such as the fire service, the ambulance service, the local authority, local businesses, local schools, local politicians etc. Can you provide an example that demonstrates that you are comfortable working with a range of stakeholders and groups?

You will be required to build confidence in the public as communities are now far more diverse than ever. During the interview you will need to demonstrate that you capable of working with other people, regardless of their age, gender, background, special needs, religious beliefs, sexual orientation or otherwise. So, can you demonstrate that you can communicate with individuals from minority communities, or those with communication difficulties?

No Garda wants to feel unwelcome in his or her own community. Being domineering or forceful only results in negative Garda relations within a community. Avoiding that vicious circle is incredibly important and every Garda needs to do their part for the community to succeed. So, can you demonstrate that you can use appropriate language and style of communication that is relevant to the situation and people being addressed?

As a Garda it is also very important that you develop strong working relationships both inside and outside of the organisation to achieve common goals. This means you should always seek to gain commitment from others by consulting and involving them in key decisions. You must understand their perspective and take this into account in your decisions and actions. Can you provide an example that shows that you consider others in your discussions and decisions?

Exercising Authority

Here is the official description of the competency:

Demonstrates the ability and willingness to take a clear and credible lead; having the self-assurance to make rapid, well-judged, and potentially unpopular decisions, executing and standing by them.

Why is Exercising Authority important to the role of a Garda Trainee?

The panel is looking for evidence that you are comfortable taking ownership of a challenge and can make balanced judgements about the correct course of action to take.

It is extremely important for Gardaí to make decisions. It can sometimes be a difficult job, which therefore requires a calm, logical and reasonable approach to the challenges you may face. It is hugely important that your decision is not influenced or compromised by personal values, relationships, or any other bias.

It is important to be always professional. Gardaí are role models for the public, and therefore it is essential that they can act in a professional and responsible manner, with integrity and in line with An Garda Síochána Code of Ethics.

Remember that your primary duty is to the public and therefore your decisions should be made in the best interest of public safety. During your response to the interview questions, make sure you show how you arrived at your decisions and the positive impact they had on the scenario.

Be prepared to demonstrate that you can make difficult decisions under duress or stress. Did you make this decision based on logic and well thought out reasoning? This is especially important as you must be able to justify your choices and understand when the time is right to seek guidance or help on a decision.

Conscientiousness

Here is the official description of the competency:

Operates diligently, honourably, and proactively; getting work done to the required standards and putting in effort. Demonstrates professionalism and persistence; being motivated to do the right thing and seeing tasks through to the end, despite adversity.

Why is Conscientiousness important to the role of a Garda Trainee?

The panel is looking for evidence of your ability to deal with an issue, ideally by doing more than expected of you. Good examples will often involve you going beyond what the average employee in your place of work would be expected to do.

A Garda naturally reports to a superior, however, he or she must plan, organise, and manage his own workload. The Garda must also see tasks through to completion – this is especially important for routine paperwork. Can you provide an example that demonstrates that you can work independently and without supervision?

Conscientiousness always means that the Garda is comfortable dealing with uncertainty, change, and can accept that circumstances can change on a project or an investigation, impacting the timeline for delivery of the work. Can you provide an example that shows you are comfortable with your plans changing and how you subsequently demonstrated persistence by resetting and achieving results?

Resilience

Here is the official description of the competency:

The ability to cope with a demanding workload and deal calmly and objectively with difficult situations, crises, and trauma. Demonstrates a desire for continual learning and self-development, seeking and accepting feedback from others.

Why is Resilience important to the role of a Garda Trainee?

The panel is looking for evidence that you remain positive and optimistic when setbacks occur; that you always seek to find a way forward.

With the increased public scrutiny of An Garda Síochána, it is more important than ever that they recruit resilient candidates. As a Garda you can expect exposure to potentially traumatic incidents and events. You can expect to be filmed by members of the public as you carry out your duties. You can also expect to meet angry and uncooperative members of the public. Finally, it is important to know and accept that not all investigations will reach a conclusion or cases turning out as you had planned them.

The panel will want you to demonstrate that you can recover quickly from setbacks, that you are tough minded and become even more determined when things do not go your way!

Using Information and Problem Solving

Here is the official description of the competency:

Demonstrates strong problem-solving skills with an ability to effectively assimilate and evaluate information from a range of sources to support good quality decision-making and generate solutions that meet the needs of a given situation or wider objective.

Why is Using Information and Problem Solving important to the role of a Garda Trainee?

As a Garda you must be competent at gathering information from a range of sources to solve a problem, then draw a logical conclusion and make an effective decision based on that information.

A Garda often works within tried and tested procedures and remains focused on the main issues, however, he or she must also have a keen eye to identify inconsistencies in information.

Of great importance is the Garda's ability to remain calm, impartial and avoid jumping to conclusions. One of the key traits I observed in high performing Gardaí, when I was managing a District, was their ability to break problems or challenges down into smaller parts and effectively use all the resources available to them to resolve the issue.

Finally, a Garda must demonstrate both patience and determination in resolving a problem – some investigations can be a real slow burner.

How to Close the Interview

For starters, do not ask any questions about An Garda Síochána or about the next steps. You should have researched this!

Instead, use it as an opportunity to reinforce why they should choose you. Thank the panel for the interview and explain that you hope you have demonstrated that you have the qualities, the relevant experience, and the character to make an excellent Garda Trainee.

General Questions:

After the five core competencies are completed by the interview panel, they might ask you general questions at the end of the interview. Here is a selection of questions that I typically asked candidates when I sat on the interview panel.

Why are you leaving your current job?

Note: Stay away from bad-mouthing your current employer and your boss. Focus on the positive.

"I have learned a lot from my current role, but now I'm looking to pursue a life-long dream and join An Garda Síochána. It is a hugely challenging, varied, and exciting career and I believe I have the qualities to make an exceptionally good Garda".

Focus on the attraction of a career in An Garda Síochána – variety / making a difference / promotional opportunities etc.

Where do you see yourself in five years?

Note: There is really no right answer to this question, but the panel wants to know that you are ambitious, career-oriented, and committed to a future with An Garda Síochána. So, instead of sharing your dream for early retirement, or trying to be funny, give them an answer that illustrates your drive and commitment.

What is your greatest weakness?

Note: This question is a great opportunity to put a positive spin on something negative, but you do not want your answer to be cliché – joking or not. Instead, try to use a real example of a weakness you have learned to overcome.

"I have never been very comfortable with public speaking which, as you know, can be a hindrance in this field. Realising this was a problem, I asked my previous employer if I could enrol in a presentation workshop. I took the course and was able to overcome this gap. Since then, I have given several safety presentations to school children across the county".

Why should we move forward with you Application?

Note: A good answer will reiterate your qualifications and will highlight what makes you unique.

I have also taken the time to educate myself on the role of a Garda from the training in Templemore, learning modules and being assigned to a Garda Station in Phase 3. Building a career in An Garda Síochána is a lifelong ambition of mine. I believe I have the qualities (interpersonal skills, resilience, leadership, problem solver, and conscientious) and relevant experience (insert your experience here) to make an exceptionally good Garda.

What is your greatest failure, and what did you learn from it?

Note: You do not want to highlight a major regret – especially one that exposes an overall dissatisfaction with your life. Instead, focus on a smaller, but significant mishap and how you have learned from the experience.

How do you explain your gap in employment?

Employment gaps are always tough to explain. You do not want to come across as lazy or un-hireable. Find a way to make your extended unemployment seem like a choice you made based on the right reasons (e.g., further study, travel etc.).

What if my Interview in conducted Online?

Do not panic. Everything we have covered in this Chapter still applies. Here is my checklist for preparing for an Online Interview.

- Get your location ready - you'll need a quiet room with no interruptions. Find somewhere you can sit in front of a plain background that will not be distracting. It is important to have good, natural light or use a lamp so that the interviewer can see you well on screen.

- Use a computer or laptop rather than a tablet or mobile phone.

- Position your computer so the camera is at eye level. – place your laptop on a pile of books. Headphones will improve your sound quality.

- You should do some practice runs by recording yourself and watching the recording back. Make sure that when you are talking to camera you pause at the end of a question so that you do not talk over the interviewer (there is a slight delay online)

- Keep up good eye contact – look at your camera rather than at the screen.

- If you experience any technical problems, let the interview panel know. Do not try to muddle through. It is better to stop and restart than pretend everything is okay.

Can I sit the Competency Interview as Gaeilge?

The answer is yes. Obviously, you will need to a fluent Irish speaker. As outlined in Chapter 1, you should apply in the usual way and indicate on your Application Form that you wish to apply through the Irish language stream.

Some Final Tips for the Competency Interview

1. Ensure that you have prepared yourself well in advance for the interview by doing your research on the key requirements and responsibilities of a Garda Trainee. One of the best methods of gaining information is talking to serving Gardai to find out what they do. You can do this by visiting your local Garda station.

2. Prepare specific behavioural examples that demonstrate how you fulfil each of the competencies. Use the STAR method.

3. Do not answer if you are unclear of the question! Not listening to the question is the primary reason that candidates fail the interview. Listen carefully and ask for clarification if necessary. My mantra is 'Breathe, Think, then Speak' not the other way around!

4. Manage your energy levels. Present yourself in a positive and enthusiastic manner. Be aware of your tone – do not respond in a monotone voice.

5. Keep to the point and avoid the temptation to over-elaborate and get into too much detail.

6. Maintain eye contact with the interviewers. Body language is important too. Sit up straight and do not fold your arms or lay back.

7. Avoid talking about any personal problems that are not relevant to the selection criteria.

8. Do not criticise previous employers. The interview is not about their shortcomings, but your suitability for employment as a Garda Trainee.

9. Dress appropriately. Business Attire. No compromises.

10. Back yourself. Preparation is vital – the better prepared you are, the more confident you will feel. If you prepare appropriately, you will be successful!

GardaIP offers a dedicated one-to-one session (Face-to-Face or Video Conference) on preparing for the Stage 3 Competency Interview.

Chapter 6

Numerical Reasoning

Introduction

I have decided to include a dedicated chapter to Numerical Reasoning. Numerical Reasoning has not formed part of the Psychometric Test set at Stage 1 or Stage 2 for several years. However my rationale for including it in this book is that it is always better to be prepared in case An Garda Síochána decide to include it in future Garda Entry competitions.

Ok so let's get into the detail.

What is Numerical Reasoning?

Numerical Reasoning is the ability to deal with numbers and to get useful information from them. When your aptitude is being tested you will have to show that you can add, subtract, divide, and multiply as well as work with fractions, percentages and ratios. You will also probably have to show your understanding of data in charts, tables, and graphs. These are all skills that you have been taught in school. Practice will help you remember them.

The Numerical Reasoning Test will be timed and you will have to work quickly – but accurately. Recent Garda internal promotion competitions have not allowed the use of handheld calculators during the Test but this rule may vary from competition to competition. Instead, candidates must use the calculator programme on their PC/laptop. This will cause some frustration for candidates who do not prepare. My advice is to familiarise yourself with the inbuilt calculator on your laptop / PC well in advance of taking the Numerical Reasoning Test.

Can practice improve your score?

The answer is a resounding 'Yes'! Numerical Reasoning Tests are made up of lots of different types of questions, and practice will familiarise you with the common patterns and formats used. If you are not mathematically minded, do not panic - practice will greatly boost your performance on the day.

Types of Questions in Numerical Reasoning Tests

The Test is typically found in two basic formats;

1. A series of number-based questions and calculations.

2. Numerical data shown in a table, graph or chart followed by a series of questions on the data. Tests like this also assess your ability to extract numerical information presented in various formats. This is the most common format.

A typical Numerical Reasoning Test examines your ability to locate and use information given in graphs and charts of different kinds e.g. line graphs, column charts, stat tables, or pie charts.

Whichever type of chart is used, your task remains the same – to find the relevant data and information quickly and accurately and then use it to answer the question.

My 3 Tips for interpreting Charts and Tables

1. Scan the whole graph or table before you start answering the questions.

2. Carefully read the units i.e. is it cm's, euros, meters, kms, and make sure you answer in the correct unit.

3. Always read the choices before you answer so you have an indication if you are within the ballpark range when doing your calculations.

Number-based Calculations:

Adding, subtracting, multiplying and dividing are all basic numerical calculations. It's unlikely that a question will require just these basic calculations, but they are the cornerstones of a lot of numerical challenges. Therefore you will need to use these as part of the solution.

In terms of tips for basic calculations you should use a technique called 'Estimation'. It can sometimes be quicker to round off numbers and make a rough calculation in your head than reaching for a calculator. Although this may not give you the exact answer, it may get you close enough to see which of the multiple choice options is the correct answer.

For example, you may have to calculate 51 x 19, a difficult calculation to do in your head. Your options are a) 245 b) 591 c) 969 d) 2115 and e) 3001. 51 and 19 are close to 50 and 20, so a quick way to solve this question would be to work out 50 x 20 in your head (1,000), then select the option closest to 1,000, which in this case is 969.

More Advanced Numerical Calculations:

As mentioned the basic numerical calculations are hygiene factors – the reality is that the most common types of question in numerical reasoning tests are *averages, percentages, and ratios.*

I will cover each of these individually now.

Averages:

The average, or mean, of a number of values is simply the sum of the values divided by the number of values e.g.

Q: What's the average of 8, 6, 13 and 25?

A: (8 + 6 + 13 + 25) / 4, so the average of these numbers is 13

In another type of question you could be given the average and all but one of the values and asked to calculate the missing value.

Q: What is the value of a, if the average of a, b, c and d is x?

A: Multiply the average, x, by the number of values that make up the average (here the number of values is 4 because you have a, b, c and d). From this subtract the values that are given (b, c and d). The remaining value is the value of a.

Formula: (x multiplied by Number of values) – b – c – d

Example Question:

Q: If the average of a, 12, 15, 10 and 30 is 15, what is the value of a?

Solution: You have to work out $(15 \times 5) - 12 - 15 - 10 - 30 = 75 - 12 -15 -10 - 30 = 8$, so the value of a is 8

Example Question:

Q: If five pieces of cheese each weigh 145g, 155g, 139g, 162g and 159g what is their average weight?

   a. 146g

   b. 148g

   c. 150g

   d. 152g

   e. 155g

A: $(144 + 155 + 139 + 162 + 159) / 5 = 151.8$ - rounded up its 152g so answer is d.

Percentages:

A percentage is a way of expressing a number as a fraction of 100 – in other words, it is a number divided by 100. Therefore, 7 per cent is the same as 7 / 100, and it is also the same as 0.07.

You must be comfortable with these transformations, because you will often need to transform a percentage, such as 10 per cent, into a decimal, 0.1, in order to make the calculations required for a numerical reasoning question, and you will often be asked to transform the answer back into a percentage.

Q: What is y% of A?

A: Divide y by 100 and multiply this by A

Formula: A x (y/100)

Example Question:

Q: What is 15% of 60?

Solution: You have to work out 60 x (15/100) = 60 x 0.15 = 9

Example Question:

Q: What is 18% of 1,500?

    a.   230

    b.   250

c. 270

d. 290

e. 310

Solution:

Apply the formula A x (y/100)

1500 x (18/100) = 15,00 x 0.18 = 270 – so answer is c

Now that you know how to work out this type of percentage calculation, all you need to do is recognise it when it is required in a question.

Look at the sample questions below, each involves different things, but essentially all that is required is for you to find a specific percentage of a given value.

Example Question:

If 200 people, of whom 40% were men, attended a Tech Conference, how many men attended the conference?

a. 40

b. 50

c. 60

d. 70

e. 80

Solution:

Apply the formula A x (y/100)

200 x (40 / 100) = 200 x 0.40 = 80 – so answer is e

Here is another type of percentage question.

Q: What is x as a percentage of A?

Solution: Divide x by A and transform this into a percentage

Formula: (x/A) x 100%

Example Question:

Q: What is 20 as a percentage of 80?

Example Answer:

You have to work out 20 / 80. This will give you 0.25, which you have to transform into a percentage, so the answer is 25%

Example Question

Q: What is 150 as a percentage of 600?

  a. 17%

  b. 19%

  c. 21%

  d. 23%

  e. 25%

Solution:

Apply the Formula (x/A) x 100%

(150/600) x 100% = 25% - so the answer is e

Here is a further type of percentage question.

Percentage Increase / Decrease

Q: What is A increased by x%?

Solution: Add x to 100. Divide this value by 100 and multiply it by A.

Formula: A x [(100 + x) / 100]

Q: What is A decreased by x%?

Solution: Subtract x from 100. Divide this value by 100 and multiply it by A.

Formula: A x [(100 -x) / 100]

Example Question:

Q: What is 20 increased by 7%?

Example Answer:

Apply the formula A x [(100 + x) / 100]

20 x [(100 + 7) / 100]

= 20 x [(107 /100) = 20 x 1.07 – so the answer is 21.4

Or

Example Question:

Q: What is 20 decreased by 7%?

Example Answer:

Apply the formula A x [(100 -x) / 100]

20 x [(100 - 7) / 100]

= 20 x [(93 /100) = 20 x 0.93 – so the answer is 18.6

Shortcut Tip:

Use this shortcut to skip all the calculations. Transform x into decimals and add 1. This has the same value as [(100 + x) / 100]. So if you multiply this directly by A, you will get your answer.

Look at the question above. Transform 7% into 0.07 and add 1, this gives you 1.07. Now multiply this by 20 and you have the answer. This shortcut takes you directly to the final calculation, which saves you time!

Watchout:

Don't get confused when the question is about an increase that is over 100%. Here's an example;

Q: What is 200 increased by 110%

    a. 405

    b. 410

    c. 415

    d. 420

    e. 425

Solution:

$200 \times (1.1 + 1) = 200 \times 2.1 = 420$ – so the answer is d.

Successive Percentage Increases:

The best way to explain this is through an example.

Q: If an organisation's revenue increase from €50,000,000 by 5% per year, what will it be in 3 years?

    a. 52,500,000

    b. 53,000,000

    c. 55,125,000

    d. 57,881,250

    e. 60,250,000

Solution:

To solve this question, you to calculate the percentage increase successively for each year.

In Year 1: €50,000,000 x 1.05 = 52,500,000

In Year 2: €52,500,000 x 1.05 = 55,125,000

In Year 3: €55,125,000 x 1.05 = 57,881,250

So the answer is d.

This is not a difficult question. It just requires you to make the same calculations a few times over!

Percentage increases from A to B:

The solution here is to divide B by A and subtract 1 from the value you get. Then you transform this into a percentage.

Formula is: [(B/A) – 1] x 100%

Again this is best explained with an example

Q: What is the percentage increase from 35 to 35.8?

Solution:

You have to work out (35.8 / 35) – 1 = 1.02 – 1 = 0.02

Transform this back to a percentage , so the answer is 2%

Example Question:

Q. What is the percentage increase from 0.75 to 1.25?

    a. 59%

    b. 61%

    c. 63%

    d. 65%

    e. 67%

Solution:

Use the Formula $[(B/A) - 1] \times 100\%$

$(1.25 / 0.75) - 1 \times 100\%$

$= 1.66 - 1 = 0.666$

Transform this back to a percentage and round up to 67% - so the answer is e

Percentage decreases from B to A:

The solution here is to subtract A from B and divide this by B. Then you transform this into a percentage.

Formula is: $[(B - A) / 1] \times 100\%$

Again this is best explained with an example

Q: What is the percentage decrease from 60 to 40?

Solution:

Apply the formula [(B - A) /1] x 100%

You must work out [(60 – 40) / 60] = 20 / 60 = 0.33

Transform this back to a percentage, so the answer is a 33% decrease

Ratios:

Ratios are used to make comparisons between two things. The most common way to present ratios is by writing 'the ratio of A to B' or by writing A:B. Note that if the ratio of A:B is 5:1, this simply means that A is 5 times greater than B.

Let's now cover the most common types of questions with ratios.

Q: What is the ratio of A to B, if A = a and B = b

Solution: Divide a by b. This quotient to 1 (i.e. :1) is the ratio of a to b.

Formula: a/b: 1

Example Question:

Q: What is the ratio of A to B, if A = 16, and B = 20

A: The ratio of A to B is 16/20:1 = 0.8 / 1

Example Question:

What is the ratio of A:B, if A = 500 and B = 200

    a. 1.5:1

    b. 2.0:1

    c. 2.2:1

    d. 2.5:1

    e. 3.0:1

Solution:

Apply the formula a/b: 1

The ratio of A to B is 500/200:1 = 2.5:1 so the correct answer is d.

Example Question:

What is the ratio of examples to test questions if there are 5 examples and 35 test questions?

    a. 0.10:1

    b. 0.11:1

    c. 0.12:1

    d. 0.13:1

    e. 0.14:1

Solution:

Apply the formula a/b: 1

The ratio of A to B is 5/35:1 = 0.14:1 so the correct answer is e.

Another common ratio question is when you are given the ratio of two groups and the size of one of the two groups, and you are asked to calculate the size of the second group.

Q: If the ratio of A to B is x:y, and B = b, what is the size of A?

Solution: Divide x by y and multiply the quotient by b

Formula: b x (x/y)

This is best explained through an example.

Example Question:

If the ratio of apples to oranges is 7:2, and there are 17 oranges, how many apples are there?

Solution:

Apply the formula b x (x/y)

17 x (7/2) = 17 x 3.5 = 59.5 or 60 apples

You may also be given the value of A, and asked to work out the value of B.

In this case you need to take this approach.

Example Question:

If the ratio of A to B is x:y, and A = a, what is the size of B?

Solution:

Divide y by x and multiply the quotient by a.

Formula is a x (y/x)

Example Question:

If the ratio of apples to oranges is 5:1, and there are 160apples, how many oranges are there?

Solution:

Apply the formula which is a x (y/x)

160 x (1/5) = 160 x 0.20 = 32oranges

Example Question:

If the ratio of males to females in a college class is 1.4:1 and there are 30 females, how many males are there?

   a. 40

   b. 42

   c. 44

d. 46

e. 48

Solution:

Apply the formula b x (x/y)

30 x (1.4/1) = 30 x 1.4 = 42males so the answer is b.

Another very common type of ratios question is when you are given the total number of a group and the ratio of its subgroups, and you are asked to find the size of the subgroups i.e.

Q: If A consists of B and C, and the ratio of B to C, is xy, what is the size of B?

Solution: Divide x by the sum of x and y. Multiply this quotient by A.

Formula: A x [x/(x+y)]

Here's a typical example.

Example Question:

If there are 400 people at a rugby match with a male to female ratio of 3:1, how many males are at the match

Example Answer:

Use the formula A x [x/(x+y)]

You must work out 180 x [3/(3+1)] = 180 x 3/4 = 135

Here is another common ratio question. You are given the value of B and asked for the value of C. Let me explain.

Question:

If A consists of B and C, and the ratio of B to C is xy, what is the size of C?

Solution:

Divide y by the sum of x and y. Multiply this quotient by A.

Formula is: A x [y/(x+y)]

This is best explained by a typical question you will encounter.

Example Question:

If there are 40 balls in a bag with a red to blue ratio of 4:1, how many blue balls are in the bag?

Example Answer:

Apply the formula - A x [y/(x+y)]

40 x [1 / (4+1)] = 40 x 1/5 = 8

There are 8 blue balls in the bag

Conclusion:

So that concludes the chapter on Numerical Reasoning.

By practising these tests you will become familiar with the typical questions, you will develop your own style of approaching them and importantly you will increase your confidence. If you are confident and rid of any anxiety, you are much more likely to perform your best. Panic and anxiety only inhibit test performance.

Practice will get you used to how much time you should spend on each question and how much working to write down - too much and you will waste time, too little and you will not be able to go back through steps in a calculation.

If you have a strong grounding in practicing the most common types of questions, you will be in great shape for performing your best at the numerical reasoning test.

Practice makes perfect! A good place to start your practice is on the GardaIP website.

Chapter 7

Frequently Asked Questions

Introduction

The focus of this Chapter is to cover the most frequently asked questions I have received from candidates through the years. I have filtered these down to the most commonly asked questions. However, if you have a question that I have not covered in this chapter, then simply contact me directly. All my contact details are on my website: www.gardaip.com.

An Garda Síochána is an ever-evolving organisation, so changes to policy and strategy can be expected and is always welcome. My responses are therefore based on the most up-to-date information available at the date of this book publication.

How long will the training take at the Garda College, Templemore?

The Garda Trainee/Probationer training programme is typically delivered over a two-year period leading to a BA in Applied Policing (Level 7 NFQ), received from the University of Limerick (UL). Training is divided into three phases:

Phase I: Phase 1 takes place over 34 weeks including a two week leave. Pre-Covid all of this training took place at the Garda College, Templemore. All Trainee Gardaí must reside in the college Monday to Friday inclusive. You will receive a weekly training allowance of €184.

You should be aware that this training period may be shortened or extended for longer periods if the Garda Commissioner deems it appropriate. For example, in 2020, at the height of the Covid pandemic, over 70 new Gardaí graduated after completing a modified training programme which focused on on-the-job experience rather than training in the Garda College.

Phase II: On successful completion of Phase I training, you will be attested and will progress to Phase II of your training. You will now be a Probationer Garda and will be appointed as a member of An Garda Síochána.

Phase II is also typically 34 weeks in total. This is the operational phase – you will be assigned to a Garda station and will work alongside an assigned Garda assigned to mentor you through this training period. From a pay perspective you will sign a permanent contract of employment and will receive a salary.

Phase III: Phase III is completely autonomous – in other words you will work independently without an assigned mentor.

What subjects will I have to study at the Garda College?

The subjects are called modules. These can change over time depending on the demands of the job. All the learning is assignment based and often group based. You must pass all exams and assessments during each phase of training in order to graduate.

The modules include:

- Foundations of Policing

- Professional Competence

- Crime and Incident Policing

- Policing with Communities

- Road Traffic Policing

- Station Roles and Responsibilities

- Officer and Public Safety

- Law and Procedures

How do I get into a specialist area such as the Special Detective Unit (SDU), Drugs Unit, Economic Bureau, Cyber Crime Unit or Water Unit?

As a new member of An Garda Síochána, you will typically spend at least three years on normal uniformed policing duties. Think about it – it makes perfect sense. You will need to cut your teeth with frontline, operational experience and work under the mentorship of your more seasoned and experienced colleagues.

After that, as you gain exposure to all the aspects of uniformed community policing, you may apply for any vacancies which may arise in specialist areas. Each section will have its own unique selection procedures.

How tall do you have to be to join An Garda Síochána?

So many candidates still think there is a minimum height requirement to join An Garda Síochána, however, the height requirement was abolished in 2001! In the past, a male Garda had to be over 5 feet, 9 inches and a female Garda over 5 feet, 5 inches.

Is there an Age limit?

You must be 18 years of age but not yet 35 years of age on midnight of the closing date for the competition to apply. You should be aware that this condition around the maximum age limit for entry is regularly challenged by applicants.

What kind of shifts will I be expected to work?

An Garda Síochána provides a 24-hour, seven day-a-week service, therefore as a Garda you will be required to work a variety of shifts associated with particular duties and locations. This includes weekends, night shifts and public holidays.

Can I apply if I wear glasses / contact lens?

Yes, as long as your vision can be suitably corrected. As part of the recruitment process you will need to do an eye test as part of your medical assessment.

I have a criminal conviction – will this prevent me from applying?

There are several factors to consider here - for example, the type of offence and the severity of the conviction. So, there is not a clear answer to this. My best advice is to include all this detail on your Application Form. You are expected to disclose everything, as failure to disclose any previous issue or prior offence history will be looked upon unfavourably and your application may be cancelled.

How long does it take to conduct background checks?

The timing for each applicant differs depending on the type of checks necessary. As would be expected, An Garda Síochána must be very thorough and comprehensive in the background checking process. The background check takes longer if you have lived abroad or have changed your residence frequently.

Will An Garda Síochána increase the ethnic diversity in the organisation?

I'm a firm believer that An Garda Síochána should reflect the diversity of Irish society and should, therefore, develop recruitment strategies to achieve a more diverse intake. In fairness, recent recruitment campaigns have advertised and promoted a career in An Garda Síochána to attract candidates from minority communities, including the publication of video content and materials in multiple languages. There has been great progress on ensuring that the Garda uniform accommodates religious diversity. Recently, An Garda Síochána also adopted a new diversity and integration strategy which promises a commitment to further diversity in the Garda workforce. All incredibly positive developments.

Do I have to be fit to join An Garda Síochána?

The role of a Garda can be very physically demanding. As part of the recruitment process, you will have to pass a fitness test. My advice is to start to build up your physical fitness now – trying to build up your physical fitness over a short period is very stressful and challenging!

I am currently studying and I am not due to graduate until next year. If I apply to the upcoming recruitment campaign and am successful and offered a place at the Garda Training College, can I defer my start date?

You can apply to the current recruitment campaign when it opens. If you are successful through all stages of the recruitment process and are offered a place in training at Templemore, my experience has been that An Garda Síochána are open to liaising with you and will consider all deferral requests. I know from preparing candidates through the years that An Garda Síochána considers all deferral requests on an individual basis and any arrangements for deferral are typically time bound.

Do I have to work weekends, holidays, unscheduled overtime, and nightshifts?

An Garda Síochána operates 24 hours a day, 365 days a year. As a result, Gardai are required to work shifts at unusual times.

How long after the recruitment campaign announcement will Stage 1 will commence?

Typically Stage 1 takes place five to six weeks after the announcement of the campaign. It typically runs over a two-week period.

What can I do now to prepare for the recruitment process?

Research the role online, talk to serving or retired Gardaí, exercise, and keep fit.

It is on you to know all about the role you are applying for. Take ownership of it. There is a wealth of information online (including reaching out to us at www.GardaIP.com). If you understand all the stages of the recruitment process and have practiced and prepared for each stage you will significantly boost your chances of success.

A Final Word

A Final Word

"Whether you think you can or think you cannot, you are right"

Henry Ford

Ford is right, we are the ones who determine whether or not we are successful through how committed we are to the idea that we can succeed. Those who believe they cannot do something will not prevail.

So, as we close out this book, let us talk about mindset. At GardaIP, we have been preparing applicants for a career in An Garda Síochána for over 15 years and 99.9% of the time we can identify the applicant that will succeed at every stage of the recruitment process.

So, what sets that applicant apart from others? You have got it... mindset. Let me explain.

From our experience, this mindset comes down to your attitude. From the very outset of the Garda recruitment competition, being optimistic and positive in your approach is a major advantage. Let me give you a real life example.

Last campaign I got a call from a candidate (let us call her Mairead) and she was concerned about the Logical Reasoning Test. She told me she was a poor maths student in school and "goes to pieces when faced with those kinds of problems to work out". These are just hang-ups we all carry - we all have them and they serve no purpose! Instead, we turned the conversation to solution mode.

I asked Mairead what she planning to do to face this challenge. I advised her that she must approach it with confidence and a positive mindset. We talked through a typical Garda Entry Logical Reasoning Test set by the PAS. I told her that she can learn in advance how to systematically analyse and breakdown complex ideas, identify the common pitfalls, and most importantly be organised and relaxed when sitting the Logical Reasoning Test. In other words, there is nothing that cannot be learned through dedicated hours of study.

Not only did Mairead smash the Stage 1 Assessment, but also placed remarkably high on the Order of Merit after Stage 2. She flew through the other Stages and entered the Garda College at Templemore the following February.

Mairead had grit - this is the most important step in building a positive mindset. She was totally committed to her goal of joining An Garda Síochána. She let go of all her limiting beliefs and channelled her energies on reaching her goal - she firmly believed it was possible.

Now is the time for you to start building your positive mindset. Let go of all limiting beliefs and start to visualise yourself in the job! Channel your energy into reaching your goal of becoming a member of An Garda Síochána. Build a solid foundation through preparation today – no half measures! Remember, I will provide the guidance and directions, but you are driving the bus.

Go after your goal with the mindset that you will achieve your dream career of joining An Garda Síochána.

It will happen for you.

Noel McLoughlin

Resources

Preparation Courses

This book explains the rationale and concepts involved at each stage of the Garda Recruitment process in as simple a manner as possible.

GardaIP (www.gardaip.com) has prepared thousands of applicants and serving Gardaí for the Assessment Centre and Competency Interview through the years. Applicants often ask if they should purchase a preparation course. This question depends on the applicant.

People have been getting into An Garda Síochána for a very long time without the assistance of a book like this or purchasing a preparation course. On the other hand, for every Garda recruitment campaign, only one in ten applicants are successful. Yes, unfortunately nine out of ten applicants are unsuccessful.

A person's preference regarding the amount of preparation they choose to undertake is really the deciding factor. Some people may pass assessments without preparation. Others may struggle despite their natural ability.

A preparation course is something you will decide to purchase depending on how confident you feel about the process, how thoroughly you wish to prepare, and how determined you are to avoid failing. The choice is ultimately up to you. You can find out more about our courses at www.gardaip.com.

To sample some of the excellent content we have on our site, you can download a free guide for recruit applicants and sign up to receive expert videos that will support you in your journey to becoming a member of An Garda Síochána.

Our Courses

Application Form Assistance

As the numbers of potential candidates are so large, your application is your first opportunity to stand out from the crowd and should be carefully written. GardaIP can help maximise your application to best showcase your skills and abilities.

Stage 1 Assessment

Our Online Tutorials will prepare you with total confidence to be ready to take the Assessment Questionnaire and the Garda Aptitude tests (Verbal & Logical Reasoning).

Stage 2 Assessment Centre

Our Online Tutorials will prepare you with total confidence to be ready to sit the Garda Aptitude tests (Verbal & Logical Reasoning), Job Simulation Exercises, and Report Writing.

Stage 3 Competency Interview

GardaIP offers a dedicated one-to-one session (Face-to-Face or Video Conference) on preparing for the Stage 3 Competency Interview. Remember, you will be interviewed by the Garda Selection Board as an individual, not as a group.

Garda Internal Promotions

GardaIP offers a dedicated one-to-one session to prepare you for internal promotion – Garda to Sergeant, Sergeant to Inspector, and Inspector to Superintendent. We also prepare candidates applying for roles in Specialist Sections, Detective Units, National Units etc.

Testimonials

Here's a sample of the positive feedback we have received through the years. As the only Garda Career coaching company founded and managed by an ex senior Garda officer, our expertise and reputation is unmatched in the market.

I want to say a big thank you Noel for the courses for both the online assessments and final competency interview. Completing both of these and putting in the hours made such a difference! Get yourself on these courses!!!!

Brian Smith, *Dublin*

I bought each of the GardaIP courses, from the Application Form prep to the competency interview, and I really would not have been successful without Noel's guidance. I started my training in Templemore last March. Thank you so so much Noel, you've helped me fulfil my dream!

Mairead Walsh, *Waterford*

I used GardaIP in 2014 to join the Guards and I was successful in my first attempt with their support. I have recently worked with Noel to apply for promotion to Sergeant. I had used other providers in the past but none are equal to the support that GardaIP offers. Noel is a past member of An Garda Síochána and just gets it. He understands the job. I have, and will continue to recommend that everyone use GardaIP whether you are looking to join or get promoted. I couldn't have done either without them.

Neil Mills, *Cavan*

Noel McLoughlin is the perfect mentor; his guidance & reassurance is first class. Noel's wealth of knowledge & experience provides an insightful perspective on how to tackle the Stage 1 and Stage 2 assessments, which is incredibly reassuring during such a nerve-wracking time. Supported by all his wonderful tutorial videos and practice tests, GardaIP highlights key considerations and structures for approaching the assessments which is an incredible confidence boost on the day. As an ex Superintendent, Noel is on top of the most up-to-date challenges in the job, so you really feel you are in good hands! I highly recommend GardaIP!

Laura M, *Mayo*

Excellent preparation materials from GardaIP that helped me pass both Stage 1 and Stage 2 Thanks for all your guidance Noel. You are a fantastic inspiration and were always available on the phone if I was stuck on any aspect of the course. Your past experiences as a Garda are so interesting too – you should write a book!

Aidan Hanratty, *Limerick*

If your serious about joining An Garda Síochána, then Noel McLoughlin is your man! I joined a few other companies claiming to help you pass first time but no joy so I signed up for GardaIP's free content and honestly the amount of information available is amazing. Noel is a talented person with loads of knowledge about the Guards; he will get you through each stage but remember you have to do the leg work and be serious about joining. I got through the full process on my 2nd attempt and I couldn't have done it without Noel's help! Definitely worth every penny. Thank you so much Noel. This is my dream come true!

Jazek Pizybylsti, *Dublin*

This is the course you need to obtain clear, concise guidance on how to pass the Garda Competency Interview. Don't take it for granted that STAR is the way to succeed. It isn't. Noel clearly outlines the best way to structure answers, be confident and successful. I passed first time. I'm just waiting now for the results of my background check. Thanks Noel and GardaIP.

Mags Harkin, *Laois*

Having purchased other preparation courses over the years and failed, Noel's course was invaluable in calming my fears and putting me in the right kind of mindset to get through the Psychometric Tests. The fact that the courses were able to be put out so quickly despite the new format just goes to show how tuned in to the recruitment process Noel is. You'll be hard-pressed to find a better alternative. Believe me - I've tried, and those other courses simply don't compare!

I never bought the Interview course because my background is in HR, but made use of Noel's free material and, most importantly, the free advice that Noel provided over the phone (he takes calls!). With that in mind, the value for money is incredible.

Eamon Byrne, *Kildare*

I would highly recommend GardaIP for anyone that is serious about joining the Guards. I did an individual course with Noel and I have no doubt that his interview techniques and tailored responses ensured I was confident doing my interview.

Michelle Heslin, *Leitrim*

I would highly recommend the courses offered by GardaIP to get yourself prepared for the Garda recruitment campaign. It gives you the best opportunity to perform on the day. I've no doubt that I would not have passed each stage without the help from Noel.

Donal Coffey, *Dublin*

I was unsuccessful the first time I applied. Next time I took a different approach. I contacted Noel and he gave me excellent advice about how to approach it next time round. Not only was he available then but I regularly contacted him all the way through each stage for advice and encouragement. He is so approachable –dead sound.

Jennifer Deasy, *Meath*

Your one-to-one course Noel was invaluable – I was very confident approaching the final interview. Everything we prepared came up!

Denise O'Keeffe, *Cork*

I'm now based in Dublin city centre working in Community Policing and I love my job! My brother, a detective in Coolock, recommended Noel – he was his Superintendent when he first joined. GardaIP prepared me all the way, Stage 1, Stage 2, and Stage 3. If you are serious about joining An Garda Síochána I would recommend Noel and GardaIP.

Graham Reid, *Kilkenny*

For anyone considering choosing someone else for preparation – don't! One-to-one coaching for the Stage 3 Interview is the only way to do it. All of the preparation is tailored to your experience instead of a general copy and paste approach. I placed no. 4 on the OOM (Order of Merit).

Adam Storey, *Wexford*

I would have been lost, Noel, without your one-to-one interview preparation course. I was so well equipped and prepared.

Alan Peppard, *Cork*

If you are serious about joining the Guards I would definitely recommend this service. I even spoke to Noel the night before the interview for a final run-through. A personal thanks to you for ensuring I got over the biggest obstacle.

Michael McLoughlin, *Sligo*

I'm now a Garda trainee thanks to GardaIP. I thought I was prepared until I spent a half day with Noel. I'm in no doubt that his interview techniques and sample questions ensured my success.

Ben Gallagher, *Dublin*

I have recommended GardaIP to all my friends considering a career in the Guards. Noel spent a great deal of time with me teasing out practical examples to demonstrate my suitability. I'm now finished my training in Templemore!

Bobby Grealis, *Mayo*

GardaIP is a fantastic service. I would strongly recommend contacting them before sitting your interview. Noel has interviewed Garda applicants at the public appointments service in the past. He knows exactly what the panel is looking for. That is why I chose Garda IP.

Brian O'Toole, *Galway*

The ability to sell yourself is essential in an interview. GardaIP laid the foundation for my success. Noel spent a great deal of time coaching me on relaying relevant and specific information to the interview board.

Ultan Mulleady, *Roscommon*

I applied for the Guards in 2019. I'm not originally from Ireland; I felt a little overwhelmed by the process and all the stages when I looked into it. I contacted GardaIP and Noel really put me at ease. He's a great listener and so generous with his time – no charge! The information I received was great. After that I knew I was in capable hands with GardaIP. I used them for each of the stages and yes I'm now a serving member.

Grigore Mihali, *Dublin*

I passed first time with great scores. You also have to put the effort in. The process is about practice it's not a given. GardaIP has amazing material for Stage 1 and Stage 2 to get you practicing.

Jen O'Malley, *Wicklow*

Lightning Source UK Ltd.
Milton Keynes UK
UKHW022138100222
398499UK00006B/89

9 781914 225765